STUDIES IN MODERN EUROPEAN LITERATURE
AND THOUGHT

General Editor:
ERICH HELLER
*Professor of German
in the University College of Swansea*

VERHAEREN

Also published in this Series

Arturo Barea: UNAMUNO
E. K. Bennett: STEFAN GEORGE
W. H. Bruford: CHEKHOV
Roy Campbell: LORCA
J. M. Cocking: PROUST
Hugh Garten: GERHART HAUPTMANN
Hans Hammelmann: HOFMANNSTHAL
Rayner Heppenstall: LÉON BLOY
H. E. Holthusen: RILKE
P. Mansell Jones: BAUDELAIRE
M. Jarrett-Kerr C. R.: MAURIAC
Janko Lavrin: GONCHAROV
Rob Lyle: MISTRAL
Richard March: KLEIST
José Ferrater Mora: ORTEGA Y GASSET
Iris Murdoch: SARTRE
L. S. Salzberger: HÖLDERLIN
Elizabeth Sewell: PAUL VALÉRY
Cecil Sprigge: BENEDETTO CROCE
Enid Starkie: ANDRÉ GIDE
J. P. Stern: ERNST JÜNGER
Anthony Thorlby: FLAUBERT
E. W. F. Tomlin: SIMONE WEIL
Martin Turnell: JACQUES RIVIÈRE
Bernard Wall: MANZONI

Other titles are in preparation

VERHAEREN

BY

P. MANSELL JONES

BOWES & BOWES
LONDON

First published in 1957 in the Series
Studies in Modern European Literature and Thought
by Bowes & Bowes Publishers Limited, London

Printed in the Netherlands
by Joh. Enschedé en Zonen, Haarlem

CONTENTS

I . . . . p. 7

II 16

III 21

IV 26

V 31

VI 40

Epilogue 49

Appendix 57

Biographical Notes 61

List of Published Works 62

Select Bibliography 64

I

To proclaim a poet 'great' is often but to pay a compliment to our taste before enough time has elapsed to enable us to discriminate between spontaneity and judgment. The enormous success which the poetry of Verhaeren enjoyed before the wars was due, it has been said, to its passionate universality of outlook. Why has it ceased to affect us with the same degree of enthusiasm? The explanation may perhaps be suggested by a comparison. 'Hugo, c'est un très grand poète', Verhaeren used to say in the days when the *œuvre* he admired was regarded with an indifference from which we now watch mysterious portions emerge into the light of tolerant scrutiny. And if since his death in 1916 the poetry of Verhaeren has also suffered partial eclipse, its fall from plenary grace may be due in part to its having developed too far in the direction of Hugo's mechanical optimism. None of his affirmations have the facility of that phrase from *Les Misérables*: 'Science will remake Eden by $A + B$'. But such fatuity is corrected in Hugo's case by a sense of the night of doubt, an imaginative curiosity about the cosmic horror that envelopes existence with obscurity and hazard, which many of us find of more interest than his assurances about the inerrancy of human endeavour.

The chill of the void, the dread of the absurd afflicted Verhaeren in his turn, but within definite limits at the point when his maturing aspirations crashed (to adapt a phrase of his) like the tower of a church on fire, in the physical and mental breakdown that produced the second phase of his work. Recovering from the loss of his former faith, he could look forward to utopia but not beyond:

Futur vous m'exaltez comme autrefois mon Dieu.

It is unlikely that so naïve an aspiration will ever again inspire the degree of confidence vested in it by thousands before the complacency of this century's dawn succumbed to an epidemic of hot and cold warfare. Yet if suspension of disbelief in the grounds for such a faith can persuade us to inquire how Verhaeren came to hold it, we may perceive, not a pathetic assumption of superannuated perfectionism, but the beauty of a life dedicated to an intelligent enthusiasm for all the good works of man, and ultimately absorbed in attitudes of affirmation supported by a generosity of heart, a nobility of nature that earned for the author of *La Multiple Splendeur* the reputation of being, among the celebrities of the first decade of this century, the most beloved personality in Europe.

Even if all hope in the future turns out to be fallacious and civilization crumbles under the strain of disequilibrium between the vertiginous advances in knowledge and the stalemate in morals, we may still have time, while society holds together, to acknowledge the last positive faith in humanity to be professed in verse after men had forsaken the last of the gods. What it would be illogical to refuse to admire is the trait that distinguished Verhaeren among the poets of the Decadence: his unique fervour for life. If work so largely free from metaphysical abstraction cannot qualify as 'existentialist', Verhaeren is none the less and essentially a poet of existence, by far the most passionate singer of life to have used the French language since Hugo. In him and for him poetry and life were one. Even a man of religious conviction like Henri Ghéon could write, 'There is no finer poetical career than that of Emile Verhaeren'.

The admission that his poetry has lost much of its prestige will clear the ground for inquiring which aspects of his art and beliefs have enough vitality left in them to await a reversal of taste that may bring a fresh acceptance. The offer made in one of his best known lyrics to reveal with what exultant sympathy a poet saw the struggle of his day, his effort to match mechanical achievement with odes of ingenious imagery and unprecedented rhythmic velocity are both flawed by a relative impercipience to the menace involved in the inventions to which poets since his time have become almost neurotically sensitive. Verhaeren's sense of prediction is less realistic even than Hugo's; his notions of the conquest of the air, for instance, are far more summary and vague than the dythyrambic prognostications of 'Plein ciel' in *La Légende des siècles*. The difference brings to mind a further example. In a room in the handsome suite once occupied by Hugo in the Place des Vosges and now stored with trophies and mementos, there hangs a picture which shows the ominous ascension over a peaceful landscape of a mushroom-shaped cloud bulging with poisonous colorations–a harrowing piece of unconscious foresight. On Verhaeren's future paradise no bombs fall. His scientists scrutinize atoms; they have not yet split one.

It was not the burden of armaments but the problems of society in an age of rapid industrial expansion and ruthless competition that claimed priority of attention in the years

8

before 1914. The cold war of the time had lasted so long that swords, it was assumed, might yet be beaten into ploughshares and gun-carriages serve to bear the last of the marshalls to their graves. Meanwhile our hideous factory-towns ground wealth out of the mechanized toil of the 'slaves of labour', recruited through a costly form of magnetism called the flight from the land. On this situation Verhaeren impinged a magnifying energy of vision; from it he extracted the series of violent impressions which brought him fame. If the morbidity and neurasthenia from which he had not completely recovered when he composed *Les Villes tentaculaires* still darkened the hues and deformed the outlines of what he saw into a series of macabre hallucinations, these were pierced with shafts of sympathy and tentative rays of hope. And it was this blend of feeling and vision, this revulsion from industrial man's predicament, expressed by an imaginative realist whose moral sensitiveness had been sharpened by personal suffering as if in preparation for this vicarious projection, that moved the hearts and stirred the imaginations of pre-war readers.

Along with its truly spectacular appeal the poetry of Verhaeren had another provisional advantage. Since the death of Hugo the French muse, never for long content with esoteric refinements, could count no eminent poet (except Verlaine) whom even the intelligentsia were able to read without initiation. The Flemish author of *Les Villes tentaculaires* wrote a language which, far from being the French of Paris, was often uncouth but rarely unintelligible; he favoured free rhythms and types of verbal imagery which could be transposed into other languages without losing all their force and singularity. Served by these assets the common urgency of his theme made him the most widely translated poet of his time. When after the outbreak of war he toured the cities of Britain and of France on a mission for his country's restoration, Verhaeren found he was moving among friends, most of whom had already sought him in his works with a curiosity and an affection felt for no other poet in Europe. And when his mission was cut short by the fatal accident at Rouen station, in all countries allied and hostile alike laments and acclamations rose at the loss of a visionary who had pleaded the cause of co-operation with all the more urgency because he had portrayed with premonitory acumen whole populations trampling the harvest in flight from shattered homesteads and deserted horizons.

To the collective problems of his time in its visible manifestations Verhaeren reacted directly, and spontaneously. The courage of his response struck those of us who remember his era as heroic. But today we may pause and ask: Is it not precisely the immediacy of his reaction to a problem which could be so vividly externalized that accounts for the neglect from which his poetry has suffered in the interval? For reasons one could not attempt to analyse here, that portion of the intelligentsia who still read verse have turned more and more from a lyricism of direct and expansive communication to a poetry of hermetic symbolism and subjective metaphysics. Perhaps the explanation of this change of mood lies mainly in the acute realization, imposed by advances in psychology, that the most pressing problems of the outer world are but projections of inner stresses and spiritual disorders that call for attention at obscure levels. In any case descriptive impressionism, of which there was a glut before the wars, has ceased to be appreciated as a poetic mode on the page: its place is in the cinema.

A poet's attitude is not a matter of choice. Otherwise we might without crudity risk the suggestion that, in pursuing a line that had passed through Hugo and Zola, Verhaeren made an immediate effect on readers of his time, thereby foregoing what have since become the dominant lines of development –metaphysical exploration on the one hand, surrealistic automatism on the other. Verhaeren was not a poet in search of a transcendental formula, but he had an ethic worth formulating– one as vital and positive as any existential ethic of today. Having nothing of the contumacious irony or of the ambiguity exploited in various degrees by his contemporaries, in the spheres of feeling and vision he had a subtlety and a breadth of his own and he was by no means devoid of power of thought.

From them all he differs conspicuously in the continuity of movement which carries his development as a poet through well marked phases of personal experience and technical experiment. The inward-winding spiral typical of so much of the self-engrossed work of his time appears only in a single phase of his work. But when, having climbed out of the vortex of neurasthenia in which he had perceived himself revolving in a circle of near-insanity, Verhaeren set his feet on what terra firma his time could offer, he launched out on a line of vicarious activities, sustained by the realization that 'le monde est malade aussi', and he diagnosed its maladies as a traditionalist.

For unlike most modern French poetry Verhaeren's springs direct from the roots of his stock and soil. His inspiration is anchored in the river-bed of Antwerp, the port of his *petit pays*, from which he will set out to sing of 'stars and men'. The birthplace and its environment of water, plain and sky, the middle-class home with its pious observances, the movements of the villagers at their traditional tasks determined the native shape of his genius, and reminiscences of them persist in many of his themes, attitudes and mannerisms–local influences of a quality not dissimilar from those that shaped the youth of Alain Fournier. The intimate lure of Sologne, the *pays de rêve*, may seem at first to have been more subtle in its effect on that other genius lost to French literature in the war of 1914. But what incomparable vistas of transfiguration will arise for the dreamy young Fleming out of glimpses of the undulating plains stretching to infinity beyond the huge sweep of the Scheldt:

A l'horizon, par où les longs chemins perdus
Marchent vers le matin, à la lueur des chaumes,
Flottent, au son du vent, des formes de fantômes
Qui rasent les gazons de leur pieds suspendus.

Car c'est l'heure où, là-bas, les Anges, en guirlande,
Redescendent cueillir, mélancoliquement,
Dans les plaines de l'air muet, le lys dormant,
Le lys surnaturel qui fleurit la légende.

His life-long devotion to Flanders began from the moment his eyes opened with awareness on the village street in Saint-Amand near Puers, where on the 21st May, 1855, he was born in a large old house a few steps away from the banks of the stream. To give an idea of the scene I cannot do better than quote from some notes put together thirty years ago after a walk round the village in the company of the poet's clerical admirer, Abbé José de Smet.

'The *bourg* of Saint-Amand, now numbering some five thousand souls, consists of two narrow cobbled streets which meet at a crossing dominated by a great crucifix, still, as in the poet's childhood, gazing over at the house where he was born. Lately divided into tenements, the house has quite lost the character it once possessed. But the last house of the row retains the autonomy of its broad, many-shuttered façade, just as when occupied by the poet's uncle, one of the village magnates. The upper end of Saint-Amand approaches the river at the church; the lower is separated from it by a meadow whose surface is broken by a mound, once the base of an old windmill, a favourite subject with local painters. Looming mysteriously aloof between village and stream, its melancholy outline haunted the poet throughout life, rising from the depths of his memory to offer an appropriate symbol for the expression of many a sombre and alien mood. The huge winding Scheldt was likewise never far from his thoughts. When as a child he was not dreaming on its banks he would spend hours at the upper windows of his home, watching the distant movements of sailing vessels up stream and down. Its broad and stately progress through the plains, flowing from one alluring unknown to another, seems to be pursued and prolonged through the whole of the poet's work. The great river, which he would one day celebrate as a national hero, was in a real sense the first magician of his dreams, the father of his imagination.'

The family group was made up of the poet's parents, his sister, Maria, and his mother's brother and sister, the Debocks. The sisters collaborated in running a store in part of the homestead. Behind it pulsed and snorted the engine of a small colza-oil factory, Gustave Debock's concern, which he planned to pass over to his nephew when the boy could give proof of accountancy. The poet's aunt, Marie Amélie, seems to have inspired the deepest and most lasting affection he felt for a member of his family. All the perplexities of childhood were brought to her; she heard his confession before it was made to the priest, and his memory of her remained a unique revelation of humble piety and natural goodness. 'Toute mon enfance est restée pendue à ton cœur', he wrote in a moment of grateful reminiscence. Gustave, the poet's father, was considered something of a stranger in the land. Having left Brussels, where his father had made a modest fortune as a cloth merchant, he had married one of the Debock sisters and now lived in retirement at Saint-Amand. It has been suggested that there were traces of Dutch and Spanish blood in Verhaeren's ancestry; but he was content to call himself Flemish. At home nothing but French was spoken; an effort the boy made to learn the native language from the village schoolmaster bore no fruit.

The future poet was brought up in an atmosphere that was conventionally but sincerely religious. His father and his uncle were both actively interested in the Catholic cause. About three miles from Saint-Amand lies the pretty village of Bornhem with its monastery of Cistercians. Once a month Gustave Verhaeren would set out, accompanied by his son when the latter was at home, to visit one of the superiors of the establishment. The pilgrims would leave before dawn to arrive in time for confession and communion. A fortnight after the boy's first communion (18th March, 1866), he had been installed, despite clamorous protests, as boarder in the Catholic College of Saint Louis at Brussels, where his sensitive, impetuous nature, still in revolt against the idea of leaving home, turned him into an unruly pupil. Transferred a couple of years later to the Jesuit College of Sainte-Barbe at Gand, he became, though at times 'explosive and rowdy', docile to routine, believing himself to be in a state of grace. The basic instruction provided by the College was humanistic, and it was here Verhaeren acquired his taste for Virgil and for Racine, whose plays attracted him to a type of genius opposed to that which he is beginning to feel his own.

By 1874, his schooldays over, the exuberant youth was approaching the freedom of his twentieth year. He visited Paris for the first time and was excited by the display of Rubens at the Louvre. If it is true that his parents had thought of dedicating their son to the priesthood, that ideal had by now been abandoned along with the scheme for turning him into a *rond de cuir* in the oil merchant's office. All resistance yielded before the young man's apparent desire to study for the bar. He went to Louvain where, before long, concentration on the Pandects was outrivalled by intensive study of the arts. He now began to compose in earnest under the encouraging glances of the professor of French literature, M. de Monge, of whom he has left a grateful impression in *Parmi les cendres*. At Louvain, writes Gilkin, a fellow student also dedicated to the muse, 'Verhaeren worked at his courses just enough to be able to pass the tests; for the rest he thought only of poetry'. 'Notre vie était follement joyeuse', Gilkin continues; but he may have failed to notice an undertone of misgiving in his companion's mirth. Referring in some verses of this period to the religious poetry of the early nineteenth century, Verhaeren wrote:

> Qui l'eût prédit, mon Dieu! qu'un jour, la triste aurore
> Trouverait sans échos cette lyre sonore
> Dont les doux chants berçaient notre siècle naissant?
> Qui l'eût dit, que mon cœur, dans son vol impuissant,
> Semblable à la colombe envoyée au déluge,
> Chercherait par le monde en vain un rameau vert
> Et viendrait s'abriter dans le triste refuge
> Du temple de la Muse, à tous les vents ouvert?

The mood of regret was soon over. The young poet plunged with his chums into taverns that provided the best assortment of beers on earth, and *faro*, *gueux* or *lantin* liberated floods of excited talk.

At Louvain, says his latest biographer, the adolescent lost his faith and became a poet. The remark calls for a reservation. Verhaeren remained a believer to the end. In such fervent souls as his, the transference from the divine to the human is rarely, if ever, completed. If the 'superstitions' of the cult are shaken off, the poet's respect for Catholicism never wavers. Again and again he will revert, often in tones of longing, to the lost faith of his childhood, the ardour and beauty of whose idealism nothing can uproot from his heart and sensibilities. M. de Poncheville has speculated on the possibility of two religions, an old and a new persisting side by side in such a temperament. And it may be that critics have not given sufficient attention to the probable clash of appeals or confusion of spiritual directions, when attempting to deal with the psycho-physical breakdown which produced some of Verhaeren's most distinctive verse. A sonnet written as early as 1878 contains the line:

Telle aussi dans mon cœur où le terrible doute . . .

The tone is Baudelairean, but it might be difficult to find so direct a hint in *Les Fleurs du mal*.

We must not however forget the most notable trait of the Flemish temperament: its mystico-sensual ambivalence. The senses were now in the ascendent: Verhaeren was at work on pieces for *Les Flamandes*. When he left the university in 1881 with the diploma of doctor of laws, his portfolio contained 'La Vachère', the best of his early poems and, like most of those just written, a mature *transposition d'art*.

Now in his twenty-sixth year, the graduate was articled to Edmond Picard, the eminent jurisconsult of Brussels, one of the last patrons of the arts to qualify as a modern Maecenas. His new protégé is known to have pleaded once; otherwise most of his time seems to have been spent at the Musée Royal, the main attraction being, not the primitives, but the painters of 'carnal and opulent life', Jordaens, Rubens and the lesser masters of genre. His own life in the capital was anything but exemplary. Rumour had it that he slept out, drank and smoked more than was good for him.

Prominent among the friends of 'the Admiral' (as Picard was called), Camille Lemonnier had recently published a couple of violently naturalistic novels, *Nos Flamandes* and *Un Mâle*. With his manuscript ready for action, Verhaeren burst upon Lemonnier and conquered his approval by reading aloud a selection from *Les Flamandes*. The poems appeared at Brussels on the 1st February, 1883, in an edition of five hundred copies. Of the few who read them, most were scandalized. Members of the poet's family were grieved as well as shocked. The *vicaire* of Saint-Amand reproved the lost sheep for having produced a book which no friend of the author could show to his sister. 'M. Verhaeren has burst like an abscess', wrote one of his first reviewers. But approval came from high quarters. Huysmans admitted that 'the old Dutchman still alive in him under the skin of the Parisian neurotic has been gripped and the impartial lover of certain tints ravished'. And Barrès commented on these 'glorious brutalities'.

II

Never had so rich a glossary of pigments been poured into a volume of verse. *Les Flamandes* is an ambitious effort to rehabilitate the vision of the old masters. But the re-presentation of Flanders, her women, rustics, pastures, sea-scapes and painters, though it throbs with 'explosions of life', is narrowly selective. It is the flesh and fruit of the great baroque artists, and especially the bacchanalia and cornucopias of Jordaens, that obsess the inflamed imagination of the young puritan transformed into the 'young stallion' of a poet who looks at their canvases too persistently through naturalistic lenses of a contemporary prescription, fixed with lubricious concentration on 'les gouges'.

The scene opens on a Rabelaisian banquet at which

> Craesbeke, Brakenburgh, Teniers, Dusart, Brauwer,
> Avec Steen, le plus gros, le plus ivrogne, au centre,

perform feats of gluttony for the length of a hundred alexandrines. The second piece, literally a 'still life', is the best of the series. The poet-painter depicts his *vachère* asleep on her bed of thick grass somewhat as Baudelaire presented his giantess, but with this difference. 'La géante' is a semi-mythological figure composed of literary reminiscences and modelled to some extent on an engraving found in an edition of *Gulliver's Travels*, whereas the Flemish cowherd might have been intercepted in any corner of lush pasture and sketched on the spot. The question of modesty doesn't arise. The vigorous wench absorbs sunshine and verdure into her somnolent pose and there is no wink from the artist. His grasp of the plastic properties of words has succeeded in keeping the whole impression under aesthetic control. Turn the page and the bias reappears with 'Art flamand', a jovial piece in short lines, in which the balance swings in favour of the wench perceived in every woman the baroque Flemings chose to paint. The piece is full of native gusto and glows with blond hair and the bloom of flesh and blood taken fresh from the masterpieces. But it also takes over that contrast between the tints of classical health and the pallor and decadence of modern humanity which is developed in the fifth piece of *Les Fleurs du mal*. Verhaeren's poem is saved by its candour and is as free from the refinements of vice as it is remote from the balance found in the canvases which it transliterates and travesties.

The volume thrives on bias and excess. For the rest there are some firm landscapes in quatrains and about two dozen genre pieces fixing within the framework of a sonnet simple effects of farm life and sea-faring. None of these are remarkable; the application of the art of Hérédia to such stubborn commonplaces suffers by comparison with the models. Restraint, absent from the rest of the series, is here too deliberate and the results are flatly descriptive.

An English comparison has been suggested between the author of *Les Flamandes* and the poet of Aldeburgh. But Crabbe's realism is direct; Verhaeren's is derived. *Les Flamandes* is a distinctive series of poems, but it suffers from a split in the author's allegiances to incompatible models: on the one hand the native exuberance sustained and controlled by the technique of the seventeenth-century paintings visible in galleries and churches; on the other the forced cerebral sensuality of modern literary naturalism in its French and Belgian varieties. Apart from some vigorous poems inspired by orgies of colour and violence unprecedented in French verse, the bias is often in favour of inferior modes such as are found in Maupassant's *Des Vers*. Nothing however can conceal the fact that a personality of singular vehemence had gate-crashed, with a volume of 'glorious brutalities' under his arm, into the devitalized coteries of the Parnasse.

Back at Saint-Amand, where the storm over the poems had subsided, the young man attended mass with his parents, one of whom was overheard to inform the family butcher: 'You see, Emile is still religious'. Yet only extreme measures could save him now. He was pressed into a pilgrimage from which it was hoped rescue might come. On the last day of July 1883 the poet, accompanied by a young cousin, reached the neighbourhood of Chimay in the Ardennes, bent on making a retreat in the Trappist monastery of Forges. Away from the world the backslider meditated on the monks' imperious security:

> . . . le terrible drame
> Du siècle athée et noir n'entame point leur foi.

Conceived in conformity with the Parnassian manner and appropriately published by Lemerre, *Les Moines* is as distinctive a collection as its predecessor, but even more rhetorical. Religious themes had been dominant in the work of Leconte de Lisle. But his attitude to Christianity was apathetic; to mo-

17

nasticism he was virulently hostile. Verhaeren's attitude is valedictory and somewhat ambiguous. In a letter written at the time of publication he confessed that he hadn't 'le cerveau assez gothique pour adorer Dieu'. But if the series lacks faith it shows no trace of disrespect: such a note would have imperilled its aesthetic sincerity by destroying its consistent tone. What feelings it reveals are admiration for the monks of old, whose gestures and attitudes are matched with forceful images, and regret for the passing of a picturesque order of the sublime. Feelings inspired by the heroic or humble figures perceived in church windows or depicted in illuminated manuscripts and murals, but still more often directly modelled on the monks of the painters, El Greco, Ribera and Zurbaran, already adapted by Gautier in terza rima which must have been known to the author of *Les Moines*. The legendary stylization is often well done. But the glory has departed: 'les moines géants' are insulted by the crowds. In contrasting heresiarchs with submissive and innocent neophytes, the poet seems to be trying his hand at protagonists for his future play, *Le Cloître*. More successful are the pilgrimages and recessionals, verbal frescoes in which the monks move solemnly, chanting vespers or returning from errands of mercy. The art of distancing at which he excels is here at its inception. But of what is actually before him he sees only the cloisters and monastic buildings. One curious sonnet is a *croquis* of the vestry.

The volume appeared in 1886, three years after most of its contents were written, and its author admitted how far they then were from him. He is said to have objected that the series contained too many well made alexandrines. One understands what this meant for a poet who was reading Laforgue's *Complaintes*, which appeared in 1885 and 1886, and was soon to join the ranks of the verslibrists. The series has received little attention, but I suggest *Les Moines* as a book for the connoisseur. The sequence called 'Rentrée des moines' is one of the most attractive of Verhaeren's early poems. Tone and style are perfectly managed and prompt the observation that since Baudelaire –and despite his mastery of a form of free verse– Verhaeren was one of the strongest artificers of that most difficult of all French stanzas, the quatrain; in it he will write some of his best poems.

Les Moines retains some interest both as a large-scale *transposition d'art* and as a record of the poet's loss, or rather change, of faith. In the final invocation, 'Aux Moines', art itself is

18

declared to offer the only altar left to modern worship; the place of the monks has been taken by the artists—a thesis that sounds less facile when Malraux puts the case.

Verhaeren's first two collections we might be tempted to dismiss, with contemporary models in mind, as exercises in outmoded styles, were it not that in vigour and substance each stands out even from those productions of the time that show a similar aesthetic attitude and share the same technique. Already certain characteristic features of their author's mode of composition appear. From the first his collections are marked by unity of design. The *sauvagerie* of his temperament, even his paroxysms of vehemence, are contained and canalized within the frame-work of a consistent volume of related poems. 'Y a-t-il une impression d'ensemble?' he asked the reader of an early manuscript. 'C'est ce que je cherche'. Each collection, moreover, while constituting a whole, is usually related to another volume in the role of counterpiece in a diptych; and in some cases a triptych or trilogy of volumes will provide for the resolution of an antithesis. It is thus probably easier with Verhaeren than with most other poets to refer a specimen of work to a phase of artistic development or to a period of life. Yet one serious disadvantage threatens the unitary method of composition. Baudelaire used it successfully in composing *Les Fleurs du mal* by contriving sufficient variety within the unit of design. Verhaeren's tone is emphatic and at the same time deficient in variety, with the result that, while most of his volumes contain effective contrasts, the stronger effects tend to repeat themselves all too relentlessly and to produce a kind of monotonous resonance which has not worn well. Maurras could refer ironically to the reiterated beat of the drum at the end of the Verhaerenian fanfare.

The Mercure edition of *Les Flamandes* and *Les Moines* includes one of the rare miscellanies in this poet's work, significantly called *Les Bords de la route*. Its main interest is technical: a collection of experiments which show a gradual abandonment of Parnassian modes in favour of freer forms of verse, conceived as ancillary to an art of impressionistic emphasis. At first (1887) the normal patterns are slightly disrupted as lines of irregular length creep into the stanza formation. Correspondingly there appears a more personal note, increasingly morbid. Something has shaken the façade of confidence with a premonitory tremor:

Ah! comme il fut dolent ce soir d'opacité,
Quand mon âme minée infiniment de doutes,
S'écroula toute
Et lézarda, craquement noir, ma volonté.

III

As the leaves of the first diptych close irrevocably, the sun-splashed whirl of the *kermesse* comes to a dead stop and the line of chanting monks disappears across the horizon into the dusk of the ages of faith. We are confronted by glimpses of a mind in torment, requiring not primary colours for the adumbration of its obsessions but the sepias, flame-reds and 'blancs soleils de lune' of nightmares touched, as Baudelaire might have said, by the wind of the wings of insanity. With *Les Soirs* (1887), *Les Débâcles* (1888) and *Les Flambeaux noirs* (1890) we reach a distinctive achievement, a trilogy capable of ranking with the most personal productions of its time.

In his commemorative *Discours sur Emile Verhaeren* Paul Valéry expressed the belief that between their twentieth and thirtieth years few poets escape an essential crisis which threatens their gifts with destruction, a combat with all the elements of contradiction which life has accumulated so far and which it imposes on their afflicted organisms. Verhaeren, he thought, must have suffered in flesh and spirit this redoubtable trial; from it he emerged 'victorious, a great poet, in a word an inventor of himself'.

The keynote is struck in the prologue, 'Les Malades'. The grinding monotony of affliction leaves only its perverse cultivation at the disposal of the patient who refuses to submit. 'Se torturer savamment': the phrase comes from a contemporary letter to René Ghil. But it is the device and talisman of these poems.

It is the powerful handling of the images, rough-hewn from a distraught perception of nature, that makes *Les Soirs* (*décors liminaires*) the most varied and the best of the three collections. Continuous exchanges occur between reflections thrown up by the torment within the brain and others dragged into the vortex from the external scene, refracted through a disarray of all the senses. Psychoanalysis of the images seems to have contributed little to the diagnosis of the malady. What we see is a powerful imagination 'stupendously distraught', strenuously building up out of its own disorder rugged structures of deliberate form. A distant hill, black against the glow, dominating the woods, crushing the plains, is a taciturn idol, and sunset a flaming holocaust offered to appease its wrath. Nightfall rears a black sepulchre overhead wherein the ancient stars burn like iron lamps; for hours the stillness holds the listener transfixed. Suddenly the tension is broken by the hammer-blows of midnight beating with the weight of eternity on his brain. Silence returns, frozen in the clutch of winter. But renewed anguish galvanizes the metallic stone itself into rocks of twisted despair. Weight, which Hugo thought of as the element of sin in the universe, has never been so powerfully manipulated as in the poetry of his successor. And yet in contrast to these ponderous hyperboles, what felicity when a fragile effect is aimed at! The cry of the bird lost in the marshes has a poignancy akin to certain notes in Whitman's great lament:

> O throat! O throbbing heart!
> O all—and I singing uselessly, uselessly all the night !

What saves the victim in the last resort, what ultimately lifts him out of the mire of the Decadence, is the will to suffer in excess:

> Les maux du cœur qu'on exaspère, on les commande.

Even though despair degenerates into madness he can still set the Absurd to poetry ('Fleur fatale'). Man is abandoned; nothing remains but to wallow in trite rationality. But note the specification:

> Plus rien, ni des héros, ni *des sauveurs nouveaux*;
> Et nous restons croupir dans la raison natale.

If insanity offers the only escape from stagnation, he will go to meet it:

> Je veux marcher vers la folie et ses soleils,
> Ses blancs soleils de lune au grand midi, bizarres.

With *Les Débâcles* (*déformation morale*) a note of irony sets in, not that of Laforgue's unsatisfied sensibilities nor the metaphysical irony of Baudelaire, but a detached sense of the irony of frustrated talent, as Valéry saw it. His crown of thorns is apostrophized thus:

> Hallucine-moi donc de ton absurdité;
> Et sacre-moi ton roi souffrant et ridicule.

Motifs of vice alternate with impulses of piety. The latter revert to childhood and are contemptuously disposed of as 'niaiseries'. But the sense of loss is finely expressed in 'Pieusement':

> La nuit d'hiver élève au ciel son pur calice.
>
> Et je lève mon cœur aussi, mon cœur nocturne,
> Seigneur, mon cœur! mon cœur! vers ton infini vide,
> Et néanmoins je sais que tout est taciturne
> Et qu'il n'existe rien dont ce cœur meurt, avide;
> Et je te sais mensonge et mes lèvres te prient
> Et mes genoux; je sais et tes grandes mains closes
> Et tes grands yeux fermés aux désespoirs qui crient
> Et que c'est moi, qui seul, me rêve dans les choses;
> Sois de pitié, Seigneur, pour ma toute démence,
> J'ai besoin de pleurer mon mal vers ton silence! . . .
>
> La nuit d'hiver élève au ciel son pur calice.

A morbid egocentricity develops until the victim is 'immensément emmaillotté d'ennui'. But out of the ferment of corruption he extracts macabre elements which he will continue to exploit until strength is gained to fling the whole complex of personal woes and phobias on to the pathological state of society.

The 'projection extérieure' begins with *Les Flambeaux noirs*. 'The day when I can live completely in a state of dreams is, I feel, almost here', he writes to a friend. 'Oh! with what joy will I kick free and rush from everything in interminable travels'. He wanders like Cain under a less definite curse, haunted, he will admit, by London–'the brutal, black London of winter', as Middleton Murry wrote forty years ago in an English journal, comparing Verhaeren to the author of the *City of Dreadful Night*. The trilogy ends with an hallucination in which the poet sees his reason floating down the Thames. Not the 'drunken boat', this time, but the raft of insanity drifting past wharves and warehouses, faintly lit with Whistlerian iridescences and those illuminated dials Verhaeren will never forget. Realism and phantasmagoria are strangely blended to the rhythm of a rapid ebb-tide:

> Ce sont des quais et des casernes,
> Des quais toujours et leurs lanternes,

Immobiles et lentes filandières
Des ors obscurs de leurs lumières:
Ce sont des tristesses de pierres,
Maison de briques, donjon en noir
Dont les vitres, mornes paupières,
S'ouvrent dans le brouillard du soir;
Ce sont de grands chantiers d'affolement,
Pleins de barques démantelées
Et de vergues écartelées
Sur un ciel de crucifiement.

En sa robe de joyaux morts, que solennise
L'heure de pourpre à l'horizon,
Le cadavre de ma raison
Traîne sur la Tamise.

Let us take a backward glance. As a series *Les Flambeaux noirs* is inferior to its predecessors. The melodramatic tension has become overstrained and the style weighted with rhetorical clichés, repetitions and heavy-going onomatopoeia:

Il bat des tas de glas au-dessus de ma tête.

The jangle of Poe's bells has been held responsible for such effects, and they are by no means Verhaeren's monopoly. Like most of his poetical contemporaries he progressed towards a distinctive form through experimental stages that owe much to the originality of a few precursors. The alexandrine quatrain predominates in *Les Soirs* as it does in *Les Fleurs du mal*. The intimate composition of the verse shows insistent variations on the technique of Baudelaire which, with its blend of plastic and musical effects, its use of reversionary stanzas and 'retours obstinés de phrases' had charged French lyricism to a maximum degree with incantation. As for the imagery of *Les Soirs*, while some of it derives from the same ritualistic sources as Baudelaire's, most of it is adapted from the natural scene in conformity with the prescription he gave of the pathetic fallacy in a short poem called 'Horreur sympathique'.

But in *Les Flambeaux noirs* another model has intervened. Here one can detect the incidence of *Les Complaintes* which helped to seal Verhaeren's alienation from the Parnassianism of his début. In its brief development the technique of Laforgue presents examples of rapidity of rhythm and diversity of stress not found in Baudelaire's. His style becomes a capricious agitato, full of ejaculations and interrogations, which enables his blend of sentiment and irony to attain that degree of the *suraigu* at which he confessed he aimed 'to save from going into a decline'. The urgent form of appeal to the reader, which appears in *Les Débâcles* and which Verhaeren will abuse, was already exploited in the dialogue style of his predecessor; while the blend of incantation and impressionism which is the distinctive feature of Verhaeren's *vers libre* must, I think, have had its prototype in the rhythmic patterns which Laforgue adapted to his purposes from popular songs and ballads.

Such comparisons refer to matters of technique only. The tone of each poet is quite distinct. Verhaeren is in earnest where Laforgue is flippant; ponderous where Laforgue is sprightly. One gets at times the curious delusion that each caricatured the style and mannerisms of the other. Here, for instance, Verhaeren pours out a spate of polysyllables, interrogations and syntactical monstrosities as if in imitation of Laforgue:

> Dites, vers quel inconnu fou,
> Et vers quels somnambuliques réveils,
> Et vers quels au-delà et vers quels n'importe où
> Convulsionnaires soleils?

And Laforgue might have prepared a reply in concocting a rhyme-scheme like the following, the facilities of which Verhaeren dropped into too often:

> Crâne,
> Riche crâne,
> Entends-tu la Folie qui plane?

And now let us take a glance forward. Verhaeren had the habit of adumbrating in one book what he would develop in another. Already the 'projection' of his distress begins to fix on tragic aspects of industrial activity and he experiments in appropriate modes of expression. Many of the motifs and images typical of *Les Villes tentaculaires* appear in the piece called 'Les Villes' in *Les Flambeaux noirs*, while *La Révolte* is obviously a sketch for the impetuous poem of the same name in the later volume.

IV

To introduce his comments on the lugubrious fantasy of the poet's reason floating down the Thames, M. de Poncheville in his recent biography uses an epigraph from Verlaine:

> Frais séjour où se vint apaiser la tempête
> De ma raison allant à vau l'eau dans mon sang.

In Verhaeren's case the cool shelter from the storm was once again the village of Bornheim, whither he used to accompany his father on their monthly visits to the monastery. There at the home of his sister, Maria, now the wife of Dr. Cranleu, the distracted wanderer was to find unexpected happiness.

In the neighbouring château de Marnix a young woman from Brussels had come to resume the lessons in drawing she gave to the countess's daughters. Calling on her friend one afternoon she met the poet. The depth of intelligent sympathy he discovered in Marthe Massin inspired a phase of exultancy. His love for Marthe became a religion, absorbing and refocussing the vestiges of the faith he had lost: 'Tu es un peu celle qui remplace les croyances tombées'. The current annotation of this transformation is preserved in the *Lettres à Marthe*, which were published in 1951. But the beauty of conjugal affection was to find its consummate memorial in the triptych of *Les Heures* which constitutes one of the rare tributes paid to the permanence of marital love by a modern poet. At the moment union was not an immediate prospect. Indeed the poet doubted whether his temperament would permit of the conventional solution. But this newly found relationship predominated over all other interests as he set out on a tour of the *villes d'art*. From Florence he wrote: 'It is not my art that preoccupies me, it is you.'

The beneficent influence appeared immediately, but distanced and disguised, in a new series of poems written, most of them, in London around the year 1890 and published in 1891. Of their arrangement he wrote to Marthe: 'mon prochain volume je le veux à la fin tout illuminé de toi.'

Les Apparus dans mes chemins is a work of mixed strands, hardly successful as a whole, though some of its contents show a new type of intimacy. Verhaeren was essentially a spontaneous poet, capable of writing superbly when directed by his sensibility. Too often, however, he manœuvres without intensity. We have noticed that his collections aim at unity of effect–unity, not uniformity. The 'ensemble' was contrived to enclose a certain variety or contrast to relieve or revive the tension. It is no criticism of *Les Apparus* to remark that the effect it aims at is dualistic–a conquest of light over darkness or, since the dualism is one of feeling, of joy over despair, of conviction over corroding scepticism. Such an effect falls within the unity of design just as do contrasted motifs in musical composition. What disturbs the impression are defects of a subtler kind, and it may be useful to consider some of them here, as they persist through much of Verhaeren's work and may have militated against the esteem with which it was originally received.

Despite the apparent spontaneity of the best pieces in this volume, the *esprit de système* is too obtrusive. Many of the effects, one feels, are prearranged, worked out and written down with more compulsion than inspiration. It is a legitimate function of art to produce an effect: all depends on how convincingly this is done. The art that conceals itself is not exemplified here; much of the effort is artificial. That the author should have told the woman who has transformed his existence that he wishes her influence to illuminate the end of the series indicates a genuine impulse. But two things mar its perfect fulfilment. In order to prepare for the poems that symbolize her advent, an introductory series of pieces is fabricated to recapitulate the motifs of his collapse and prepare a décor of gloom which the light of her apparition will dissipate. These elaborations lack the inevitability of the terrific fragments of *Les Débâcles*. Moreover the coming of the beloved is presented in a curiously ambiguous manner.

Of all insidious temptations to which some of the later Symbolists yielded one of the worst was a tendency to forsake Mallarmé's conception of the self-sufficing symbol in favour of a rehabilitation of allegory, from the facilities of which he had tried to preserve the poetry of his time. During his middle years Verhaeren experimented in a type of representation in which gigantic figures were patiently constructed to personify his *états d'âme*. A meticulous thoroughness, a laborious tautology and frequent facilities of rhyme and phrasing mar the effect of much of the first part of this volume. From being a poet of immediacy its author has become a meditative poet, and that is a role to which the form he is trying to find will never be well adapted. Sensation, which he can suggest with such brutality and refinement, disappears in entanglements of argumentation expressed with deliberate gaucherie as if in imitation of the naïve blunderings and reiterations of popular forms of literature; and the complexity of aims and technique prevents a real fusion of interests.

Les Apparus, however, is not a negligible volume. It corresponds to an all-important turning point in the poet's life and outlook; it marks a return to health and confidence from the brink of a disaster, the shadow of which is protracted over the first half of the series. Through its penumbra contrived hallucinations appear, figures that stand for defeated aspirations often with a display of verbosity, but sometimes with a touch of magic. The first piece, 'Celui de l'horizon', presents the poet's nihilism and fear of himself in quatrains of a strange resonance:

> Effrayant effrayé. Il cherchait le chemin
> Vers une autre existence éclatée en miracles,
> En un désert de rocs illuminés d'oracles,
> Où le chêne vivrait, où parlerait l'airain.

Such a tone is not recovered until we reach 'Celui du savoir', a personification of scepticism *vis à vis* modern science. For the rest, the ruminations remain sombre and only too often feebly realized until a premonition of change, a glimmer of light in the east occurs at the end of an insignificant piece ('L'Accalmie'). Suddenly the prolonged and exhausting exploitation of gloom, dementia and corruption is flooded with spring sunlight and allegory borrows imagery from legend and becomes religious in tone. Saint George descends to pierce the dragon of despond with his aureolated lance and the encircling shadows recede to the ringing of joyful bells:

> Sonnez toutes mes voix d'espoirs!
> Sonnez en moi; sonnez sous les rameaux,
> En des chemins pleins de soleil!
> Micas d'argent, soyez la joie entre les pierres;
> Et vous, les blancs cailloux des eaux,
> Ouvrez vos yeux dans les ruisseaux,
> A travers l'eau de vos paupières;
> Paysage, avec tes lacs vermeils,
> Sois le miroir des vols de flamme
> Du Saint Georges, vers mon âme!

Confronted by this apparition, the poet brings himself to judgment and is convicted of error in having dwelt so long in a morass of self-absorption, cultivating a hostile attitude to life. The ecstasy cannot, of course, endure. It is paradise compared with the inferno through which the sufferer has passed; but it is a state too unreal and too self-centred to satisfy a visionary realist and a potential humanitarian.

The concluding pieces are pious meditations in the vein of Verlaine's contrite poems in *Sagesse*. Verhaeren's are not addressed to Christ but appear to be inspired by a saintly influence from beyond life. Internal evidence points to memories of the aunt whom the poet adored when a child. But one had always suspected a fusion of influences here–the remoter one operating through memory, the more immediately beneficent being the influence of Marthe; and there is proof of this in the letters. Hence a double allegory of the 'means of grace', which leaves a disturbing sense of ambiguity. Has the man who had discarded supernatural resources turned to them again for help or has the poet had recourse to the language of the supernatural to symbolize his very human feelings? The sequel shows the latter to be true. This volume marks an effective reorganization of the personality through strong affection and the salvaging of the poet's work from the kind of degradation against which Tolstoy in a moralizing mood, but not without justice, protested.

A finer achievement in the allegorical vein is the collection of 1895, *Les Villages illusoires*. One of the most popular of all Verhaeren's works, it contains two of his best known poems. Characteristic of this series are the masterly pieces of atmospheric impressionism–the rain, the snow, silence and wind–interposed between more ambitious but not more effective studies in which the grave-digger, the bell-ringer, the carpenter and other craftsmen of his village are magnified beyond local resemblance into symbols of traditional toil and endurance rooted in the practical, humble services of humanity. This time the figures are not invented *toute d'une pièce*; they gain through being drawn from experience and interpreted with a sense of the age-long persistence and simple heroism of common types and tasks.

The first piece 'Le Passeur', has been regarded as a model of Verhaeren's *vers libre*. Against a scene of high wind and strong currents the obstinate old ferryman is presented by devices of rhythmical motifs and repetition as a figure of dogged automatism which, in its extreme humility, has an arresting pathos and a touch of heroism that survives defeat:

> Les fenêtres et les cadrans,
> Avec des yeux béants et grands
> Constatèrent sa ruine d'ardeur;
> Mais le tenace et vieux passeur
> Garda tout de même, pour Dieu sait quand,
> Le roseau vert, entre ses dents.

The Verhaerenian form comes off best, as here, in a poem of action. In the atmospheric interludes, 'La Pluie', 'La Neige', 'Le Silence', the corresponding variety of incantatory impressionism is also skilfully adapted. Never perhaps have the recurrences of climatic moods and changes been more dramatically evoked; never have the wintry gales blown through poetry in such shattering gusts as in 'Le Vent' or with so fierce a wail as in 'Novembre', another piece of high speed onomatopoeia from the accompanying volume, *Les Vignes de ma muraille*.

Verhaeren, as we have implied, had an unfortunate partiality for repeating his strong efforts. Here pieces like 'Les Pêcheurs' and 'Le Fossoyeur' revert to over-meticulous allegory and end in explaining their own symbolism in a thoroughly anti-Mallarméen fashion, after having exhausted the lexicons of misery and the tags and stop-gaps of an over-punctilious rhyming system. Just before the end however the series bursts into flame; the art of vivid, vertiginous movement reasserts itself, and our eyes and ears are caught by the wonderful virtuosity of 'Les Meules qui brûlent'. At such effects of fiery speed manœuvred with consummate command of image and rhythm Verhaeren excels.

None the less these three series, as we find them combined in the Mercure edition (*Poèmes III*), disappoint. Out of a total of forty poems, hardly half-a-dozen now seem good. They represent a transitional phase of formal experiment and are of considerable psychological interest. But despite its triumphs the personally invented form is so rigorously applied that its freedom seems illusory. Clichés abound; the rhyming is relentless and the dominant pattern is clearly not adaptable to all the purposes it has been made to serve. Its abuse dilutes the effect of its stronger applications. At every phase the advice for reading Verhaeren is to select.

V

In 1891, having returned from a tour of industrial Europe, Verhaeren met Emile Vandevelde, ten years his junior but soon to become the first labour minister of Belgium, and was brought under the spell of the German and French theories which coloured the socialism of the hour. A year later, with Edmond Picard and George Eekhoud, the poet assisted Elisée Reclus to install a Section de l'Art in the Maison du Peuple at Brussels. His practical interests were further extended by working for the reform of parliamentary representation, giving lectures at the Université Libre and helping to direct an excellent review, *La Société nouvelle*. The gravity with which its collaborators regarded the prospect for humanity may be gauged from a phrase taken at random from the first number for 1885: 'Contemporary society seems bound to traverse the horror of great cataclysms before consenting to admit the existence of the problem that confronts humanity.' It was in this spirit of vicarious anxiety that the poet identified his distress with that of the world of his time. His purgation is completed with *Les Campagnes hallucinées*. Not that these poems are the last to have emerged from the period of productive gloom. Some of them were written well before their publication in 1893. But the series should be read as it is now presented in conjunction with *Les Villes tentaculaires*, to whose fiery furnaces it contributes a background of nightmarish devastation and exhaustion. Together the volumes constitute the Flemish visionary's Waste Land, Verhaeren's having preceded Mr Eliot's by a couple of decades. The comparison suggested cannot be developed here; it would indeed be rich in contrasts. Eliot's represents the spiritual problem of his time, perceived in depth through personal types and situations. Verhaeren's vision lacks intimacy; it is focussed on collective plights and mass demonstrations. The tragedy is not presented as that of the soul of modern man but as that of a phase of civilization, about whose end the poet has at times an uncanny premonition. *Les Campagnes hallucinées* has something of the air of a deserted concentration camp.

'Your work is now becoming your way of life and not merely the production of literature', wrote Mallarmé on receiving a copy. Actually the series is a curiously composite work of art. One might call it Verhaeren's chief contribution to the modern macabre style. The murky vagueness of the scenes is deliberate and results at times in a kind of verbal 'smog' which has been much criticized. In the opinion of Remy de Gourmont—and M. Franz Hellens supports the Symbolist critic's view[1]—the great defects of Verhaeren's poetry are in language; and foremost among them is the lack of precision in terms and in design. The poet, says Hellens, intoxicates himself with vagueness as a sentimentalist does with ideals. Hence in the writing much confusion and indefiniteness, a flood of inexact words and insubstantial fustian, an enormous amount of artifice, and parts that are simply vulgar and flat. But he insists on the *trouvailles* of style and form. The new element in Verhaeren's poetry he distinguishes as *rhythm*. It is unique in French literature; it is all energy, dionysian.

Among his contemporaries Verhaeren admired Eugène Carrière and his own compatriot, Henri de Groux. Throughout the middle period of his work he cultivated veiled, sombre and *estompé* effects such as he found in their paintings. Reference has already been made to his imitation of the gaucheries, repetitions and negligences of traditional ballad technique. Here in *Les Campagnes hallucinées* he continues to choose his words, in obedience to Verlaine, 'sans trop de peine'. But, as M. de Poncheville points out, he can also bring off precise effects in the manner of Callot:

> Avec leur chat, avec leur chien,
> Avec l'oiseau dans une cage,
> Avec, pour vivre, un seul moyen:
> Boire son mal, taire sa rage;
> Les pieds usés, le cœur moisi,
> Les gens d'ici,
> Quittant leur gîte et leur pays,
> S'en vont, ce soir, par les routes, à l'infini.

In 'Le Fléau' the same critic has found reminiscences of Goya and of the *danses macabres* of Holbein's drawings. The suggestion has also been made that Verhaeren had studied pre-Freudian theories of mental disorder before inventing the debilitated figures that gibber and flit through the twilight of his pestilential plains, muttering their incoherent *chansons de fou*. All this hideous detail is organized by a faculty that fuses disparate elements and

---

[1] In a judicious essay on the poet. published with selections and illustrations in Segher's series *Hommes d'aujourdhui*, Paris, 1952.

makes the whole phantasmagoria move to a rhythm of cinematographic speed and continuity.

With the appearance of *Les Villes tentaculaires* (1895) Verhaeren's name becomes known beyond the limits of French appreciation as that of a visionary critic of the society of his time. So far he has aimed at greatness without achieving it. Here we may risk a superlative and say that the contrasted tableaux of *Les Campagnes hallucinées* and *Les Villes tentaculaires* offer the most spectacular poetic revelation that the nineteenth century projected into the century that has specialized in the film. And now that Hugo's *Les Misérables* has been shown so often, is it not time to screen Verhaeren's? He wrote serious poetry of a popular appeal, but the people no longer read poetry. Much of it is loosely made and full of high lights and strong shadows, but our contemporary wits prefer close-knit textures of an opalescent sheen. It is a poetry for collectivities, but collective humanity has turned to the cinema. Yet perhaps Verhaeren's loss is also his chance. For no one since his time has attempted to extract a visual poetry from the actual conditions of his age and present it spaciously to the general imagination.

Les Villes tentaculaires is in great part the work of a *révolté*, the reaction of a pious countryman to the desecration and depravities of the cities of industry:

> Formidables et criminels,
> Les bras des machines hyperboliques,
> Fauchant les blés évangéliques,
> Ont effrayé le vieux semeur mélancolique
> Dont le geste semblait d'accord avec le ciel.

Optimistic acceptance of the expanding powers of materialism and the insistence on a 'beauty of the modern' are far more restrained during this phase than seems to have been perceived by the poet's contemporary admirers. Resistance is strong and shows no complacency towards the conditions of capitalistic productivity. Even the praise of scientific progress with which the series ends is in strong contrast to the spirit of the volume which is sensitive and troubled with anxieties and regrets. The author is not only aware of the immense distress behind the spectacle of modern effort; he feels its aggressiveness in every fibre of his moral being and denounces its monstrosities in lyrical invectives which have the ring of sincerity–even though they are not pointed with the irony we have come to expect

33

of poetic treatments of the modern city since Baudelaire and
Eliot. More deliberately than either of these poets, Verhaeren is
concerned about the mechanization of life, work and leisure.
What fascinates him above all is an external phenomenon of
his time and of ours, a complex symptom which his synthetic
type of vision simplifies into a spectacular movement: the drift
of population from the fields in obedience to the suction of the
tentacled towns, and the reward of the captives with automatic
employments and degrading stimulations. Although the intel-
lectual elements in Verhaeren's work are by no means negligible, feeling and imagination predominate and, in the relative
absence of irony and satire, render his tone more biblical, so
to speak, than contemporary. Ezekiel is Verhaeren's precursor
and, like the prophet, he indulges in a rhetoric of denunciation
interspersed with laments for the simpler life with its restora-
tive hardness and sanity. Imprecation and impressionism vary
with perceptions of grandeur in these poems, most of which
are odal in character and free in form. 'L'Ame de la ville'
catches that effect, half real, half phantasmal, which our great
cities present–London, Liverpool and Manchester were the
models–of struggling through fog and smoke towards some
obscure objective. In the passage

> O les siècles et les siècles sur cette ville,
> Grande de son passé
> Sans cesse ardente—et traversée,
> Comme à cette heure, de fantômes!

we catch a reminiscence of those famous lines:

> Fourmillante cité, cité pleine de rêves,
> Où le spectre en plein jour raccroche le passant!

But unlike Baudelaire, here in the toils of the Octopus, though
elated with the spectacle of power, Verhaeren is obsessed with
the question Whither:

> Vers on ne sait quels buts inquiétants?

'The dream hovers above the smoke', but its outlines are vague
and the promise is obscure. To give it meaning or direction
the poet rehabilitates the old faith in a new form. The purpose
of it all will be realized in the advent of a new Christ having

the divinity of a purified humanity. Alternating with the scenes of urban activies, 'statues' of audacity, domination or failure occur, figures of prominent men, unidentified but envisaged in the spirit of Comte's cult of the *Grand Etre*. As for the coloured figures in the Cathedral windows, they tremble at the clangor of a train which drowns the anthem.

Many of the poems in this volume deserve more attention than can be given to them here. Each has individuality, though some of the themes will be taken up too often subsequently. 'Les Spectacles' throbs with an indignation as flagrant as Zola's against the vulgarity and debasement of popular exhibitionist attractions. The vicious beauty of venality is curiously idealized in 'Les Promeneuses', a piece which marks a great advance on those in which Baudelaire personifies public prostitution in abstract terms. 'Les Usines' has been justly praised for its impression of the horror of mechanized toil. But if organized labour is supine in its acceptance, the mob can react violently. 'La Révolte' catches the reckless energy of destructive insurrection in one of the most sustained pieces of powerfully rhythmed *vers libre* that the history of the recent form can show. Here indeed the movement of French verse is galvanized with a new impetuosity. Finally death in the city is symbolized by a concentration of all the poisons of industrial life in a figure that recalls the pestilential phantoms of the hallucinated fields:

> Tragique et noire et légendaire,
> Les pieds gluants, les gestes fous,
> La Mort balaie en un grand trou
> La ville entière au cimetière.

One of the curious features of Verhaeren's poetry is the way it can pass from the realistic observation of a modern town at work to a quasi-mediaeval allegory of this kind, and back again to the progress of scientific investigation. A note of confidence and power supervenes with 'La Recherche'. Discovery ransoms the errors and oppressions of the past by displacing them with knowledge. Its methods are finely appreciated:

> Avec des yeux
> Méticuleux ou monstrueux,
> On y surprend les croissances ou les désastres
> S'échelonner, depuis l'atôme jusqu'à l'astre.
> La vie y est fouillée, immense et solidaire,

35

En sa surface ou ses replis miraculeux,
Comme la mer et ses gouffres houleux,
Par le soleil et ses mains d'or myriadaires.

Chacun travaille, avec avidité,
Méthodiquement lent, dans un effort d'ensemble;
Chacun dénoue un nœud, en la complexité
Des problèmes qu'on y rassemble;
Et tous scrutent et regardent et prouvent,
Tous ont raison—mais c'est un seul qui trouve!

Here the sequence breaks into a litany in which, unconsciously perhaps, the strains of 'Blessed upon the mountains are the feet of him that bringeth good tidings' are transposed into praise of the bringer of scientific light, who prepares the consummation of effort:

. . . . la synthèse des mondes!

C'est la maison de la science au loin dardée
Vers l'unité de toutes les idées.

And what are the life-saving ideas? Force, equity and beauty, the total harmony, the dream of perfection. The epilogue, 'Vers le futur', resounds with renewed praise of the courageous advance and proclaims the victory of knowledge over superstition in stanzas that all readers of Verhaeren will remember:

O race humaine aux astres d'or nouée,
As-tu senti de quel travail formidable et battant,
Soudainement, depuis cent ans,
Ta force immense est secouée? . . .

L'esprit des campagnes était l'esprit de Dieu;
Il eut la peur de la recherche et des révoltes,
Il chut; et le voici qui meurt, sous les essieux
Et sous les chars en feu des nouvelles récoltes.

Half a century has elapsed since these exultant notes echoed in the attentive ears of 'four continents'. But the events that have intervened oblige us to ask: Was not the new faith a greater superstition than the old? For readers today the interest of this famous series is likely to be found not in the epilogue but in the contrasted impressions of effort and horror which the most powerful imagination of the end of the nineteenth century drew from the industrial scene. Actually Verhaeren's imagination was that of a *visuel* rather than of a visionary. He was essentially a man of feeling–'Mon cœur, buisson ardent, a mis en feu mes lèvres'–a man of feeling, strong in prophetic hope, weak in prophetic precision. The generosity of his hope seems to have prevented any suspicion from arising in his mind that the powers liberated by modern science would be concentrated, before the new century was half-way through, in the most frightful engine of destruction known in the history of invention. Had he survived the second world war, would not the author of the stanzas we have quoted not have been forced to agree with Sir Llewellyn Woodward who, in a recent broadcast, said: 'Since the latter years of the nineteenth century–since my own childhood–I have observed a terrible regression away from law, away from reason, away from restraint, away from hope.'

Yet Verhaeren's scientific optimism cannot be passed over as unrealistic. It is not even unreal *as feeling*; it is a form of modern faith. Scientific progress is impelled by, and in turn inspires, an enthusiasm of the kind exhibited in these poems. Faith in knowledge, belief in the power of pure science to make discoveries the results of which may turn out 'somehow good', is the conviction of millions of ardent workers today and need not imply a blind acceptance of automatic progress. Research justifies itself in the intelligence it gives of our universe as well as in the appliances with which it endows mankind. Discoveries, one feels when reading a book like Bernal's *Social Function of Science*, are positive gains that can give just gratification after exhilarating pursuits. Acclamations and rewards are merited. And let me add, if you want to get the feeling of restrained elation in achievement, go to a great laboratory, not to an Arts faculty. In this mood what right have we to be impatient with the poet who wrote

> L'acharnement à tout peser, à tout savoir,
> Fouille la forêt drue et mouvante des êtres.

It is when he adds:

> Et malgré la broussaille où tel pas s'enchevêtre,
> L'homme conquiert sa loi des droits et des devoirs.

that we suspect a fundamental error. Pure science produces no ethic to recommend the right use of the powers it can place without discrimination in beneficent or lethal hands. Of this we are far more conscious than were the seers of Verhaeren's time; and that is why 'Scientisme', the religion of science as understood on the Continent towards the end of last century, seems to us now a shallow and pernicious doctrine.

Verhaeren's thought does not progress much further in this direction. But he will frequently return to the more general form of hope, and here more than anywhere his feeling purifies and elevates his expression. The recent wars have proved not the inanity but the insecurity and inadequacy of the faith he formulates. But one can still be stirred by a fervent poem like 'La Prière' in *Les Rythmes souverains*, because its movement appropriates a passionate religious aspiration transformed into a yearning for a beneficent temporal fulfilment of man's tragic endeavour. The rhythm seems to leap past our reservations and broadens into an impulse of sincere, tremulous yet confident communication with men of a time nearer serenity than our 'hard present':

> Que bondisse soudain mon âme aventurière
> Vers l'avenir,
> Et tout à coup je sens encor,
> Comme au temps de l'enfance, au fond de moi, frémir
> L'aile qui dort
> Des anciennes prières . . .
>
> O l'antique foyer dont survit l'étincelle!
> O prière debout! O prière nouvelle!
> Futur, vous m'exaltez comme autrefois mon Dieu,
> Vous aussi dominez l'heure et l'âge où nous sommes,
> Mais vous, du moins, un jour, vous deviendrez les hommes,
> Et serez leur esprit, leur front, leurs bras, leurs yeux.
>
> Dussiez-vous être moins que ne le veut mon rêve,
> Que m'importe, si chaque fois
> Que mon ardeur vous entrevoit,
> Elle s'attise et se relève . . .

This prayer conveys that strong sense of relationship between the effort of today and the consummation of tomorrow which Verhaeren could express with an impulse so genuine that it seems to transcend the shattering disillusionments which separate his time from ours.

Practical forethought, as distinct from luminous hope, could not inspire such effects as these. *Les Villes tentaculaires* was followed in 1898 by the publication of *Les Aubes*, an experiment in collective drama conceived in the spirit of naïve optimism which characterized the socialistic thought of the first decade of this century and encouraged the belief that pacifistic propaganda could disband troops in action and noble arguments destroy armaments. Hérénien, the hero of the piece, may still have his counterparts in life. But the dawn has yet to rise on the success of their efforts.

VI

In his commemorative oration, Paul Valéry recalls having met Verhaeren hastening north from Florence, fleeing from the settled azure of Italian skies to recover contact with his native mists and rains. The subsequent development of his work shows this process reversed. After what has been called, not very properly, the socialistic phase, it broadens out and blossoms in a great variety of poems of affirmation, fragments of positivist faith and pantheistic jubilation. From this later phase cloud and shadow have so securely withdrawn that we sometimes feel the major volumes have lost a certain depth, and that their syntheses are attained too easily. There can be little doubt that the solution of their author's emotional problem contributed much to this aftermath of elation. Yet the phase of serenity is something more than euphoristic; it lasted to the end of his life and its spirit was not quenched even by the disillusionments of war. Matrimony, which he had viewed with misgivings, became a surprising source of inspiration. In the relationship itself he struck a vein rarely exploited in French, one which had preserved a freshness of interest that neither the sacred nor the profane varieties of passion could rival. The deliberate tumult of riotous images and suggestive cacophonies to which we have become accustomed leaves us unprepared for the felicities of expression that clothe these reveries and confessions with a primitive candour 'comme aux âges naïfs'. The workmanship is tenuous like that of an arabesque in which a vague design hovers through a mild fantasy of ornament. The same evanescent quality belongs to the motifs themselves, occasioned by the merest hint, glimpse or murmur of beauty. The atmosphere is that of the poet's country home; its radiance, colours and perfumes supply emblems of the inner blossoming joy of its owners:

> Le beau jardin fleuri de flammes
> Qui nous semblait le double ou le miroir
> Du jardin clair que nous portions dans l'âme.

Les Heures claires appeared in the year after *Les Villes tentaculaires* and was followed in 1905 by *Les Heures d'après-midi*, in 1911 by *Les Heures du soir*.

In 1899 came *Les Visages de la vie*, a sequence of fourteen poems in which the Verhaerenean form is completely and most beautifully realized. M. Hellens is inclined to think that Verhaeren never wrote a perfect poem. I venture to suggest that several poems as fine as any written in his time, and purged of his characteristic defects, are found in this volume. After the long period of alienation we have annotated, they represent a deep reconciliation with life and nature and intone that note of permanent joy which resounds throughout his later work. Though neither personal nor spiritual—it may even be a purely material force—the all-pervading life is felt as a reality with which it is essential to keep in touch. The poet believes it has the power to enlarge and beautify his own life and that, through intuitive contact with its eternal flow or through imbibing ever larger draughts of its energy, he will the more truly and magnificently live. The leading *motif* is the quest for this essential vitality, pursued through the ravishing multiplicity of natural forms and human impulses, the vigorous desire to grasp the source and secret of existence and to be filled with its strength. Most of the poems show the same emotional development from the fresh delight of the admiring artist to the ecstasy of the worshipper who has yielded, with an abandonment of will and passion, to the invasions of a power of infinite beneficence.

A typical experience, reduced to its simplest formulae, is recorded in 'La Forêt'. In contrast to the unimaginative person for whom a wood is a collection of trees, the poet approaches 'this wood, on which the centuries have laid their seal', with a feeling of veneration, a mind alert to all its suggestions, a memory stored with similes and associations. For him the forest palpitates with a primitive vitality expressed in beautiful and mysterious forms. They awaken a new faculty of the imagination; an unsuspected fancy appears in many passages which revive the ancient machinery of sylvan mythology–groves peopled with fauns and hamadryads under the sway of Diana–and blend with it the charms of mediaeval fairy lore.

A deeper note is struck in the desire expressed for a glorious expansion of being through imaginative self–multiplication in the diversity of natural forces:

> Multiplié et livre-toi; défais
> Ton être en des millions d'êtres;
> Et sens l'immensité filtrer et transparaître,
> Avec son calme ou son effroi,
> Si fortement et si profondément en toi,
> Que t'absorbent les vents et les orages . . .

This sensation is developed to its supreme pitch in the complete fusion and minute interfusion of the self–mind, body, blood and fibre–with nature.

> Oh, what a joy it were in vigorous health
> To have a body
> And to the elements surrender it
> As if it were a spirit.

It is interesting to note how Wordsworth's longing is transcended in Verhaeren's case by the *recovery* of the members and senses abandoned in the first fine rapture, and the re-assertion of the will:

> La fusion naquit, par un amour des choses
> Si simple et violent, que je ne sentais plus
> Battre mon cœur, sinon au flux et au reflux
> Des profondes métamorphoses:
> Je retrouvais mes mains, mes bras, dans les ramures
> Et les enlacements des vignes mûres;
> Le mont lui-même était sculpté
> Dans le bloc de ma volonté:
> Je me grisais de leur vie ample et mutuelle
> Et mes cinq sens se prolongeaient en elle
> Si loin et si profondément
> Qu'elle semblait brûler et fermenter de tout mon sang.

The dangers of pantheistic sensationalism are avoided through a conscious acquisition of strength. The contrast between this type of inspiration and the passive swoon of Rousseau's fifth Reverie is clear.

The year 1900 opens a decade and a half of unimpeded productivity. In that year appeared *Le Cloître*, a play in prose and verse, the best of the four Verhaeren wrote. A favourite contrast of types–the innocent and the remorseful–sketched in *Les Moines* fourteen years earlier, comes vigorously to life in this drama of personalities which could move audiences before the war with its vehement and tender rhetoric. It points to the tenacity of Verhaeren's youthful experience of Catholicism that the only work of his to have gripped an audience was a play which revived the 'gothic spirit' in which he thought he was deficient when *Les Moines* was published.

In 1904 came the first of several collections written in various forms of verse, mainly descriptive and unequal in value, about the life of Flanders, its legends and annals, its sand dunes, plains and gabled towns. *Les Tendresses premières*, based on memories of childhood and youth, is the most attractive, at least to foreign readers. For many of the poet's countrymen the whole series of volumes called *Toute la Flandre* with their animated patriotism, their local or historic reference, may well rival in interest any of his other works.

The special enthusiasm for painting which the poet inherited from his race became deeper and broader through continuous observation and more extensive acquaintance with the museums of Europe. Verhaeren was more than a connoisseur; he lived with pictures in his mind as if he were himself a painter. To visit a gallery in his company was a unique experience and could leave an unforgettable impression of vigorous judgment and finesse of technical appreciation. He wrote frequently, if not abundantly, on subjects of art. His critical biography of Rembrandt appeared from a Paris publisher in 1905, and studies of his national favourites, Jordaens and Rubens, were brought out at Brussels in 1908 and 1910.

The major works of this period complete the main line of development we have traced so far and confirm its strengths and weaknesses. It was customary in the days when the reputation of this 'world poet' stood high to count the three big collections, *Les Forces tumultueuses* (1902), *La Multiple Splendeur* (1906) and *Les Rythmes souverains* (1910), among the peaks of achievement in modern poetry. One hears little of them now. They represent a phase of positive serenity and technical mastery, when their author had become known as an apostle of force and fervour and addressed audiences on the values of enthusiasm. Several of the poems in *La Multiple Splendeur* present the evangel in earnest and magnanimous tones. But the deeper poetic intuitions of the time were remote from direct appeals to the moral conscience of collective man. Verhaeren was right, but only within narrow limits of application. His 'rule' was easier for a man of his own generosity of heart to live by than for the men who ran the world to practice in their competitive operations. In one poem in this series ('Les Mages'), he admits this by expressing doubt as to whether men of pride and power will ever submit to the teaching of a Child. But is there not a greater naïvety in the doctrine of salvation through fervour which he tacitly suggests as a substitute? When the outbreak of war dealt a crushing blow to all humanitarian beliefs, such ideals had no chance of influencing the course of events and proved inadequate to its needs. Nor did the poet himself long survive the outbreak of hostilities to support them with the magnetic persuasiveness of his personality and good faith.

While the three collections we refer to contain some of Verhaeren's maturest poems, not one of them can rival *Les Visages de la vie* in artistic unity or in sustained charm. *Les Forces tumultueuses*, though praised by M. Hellens, is (to use his test) not a volume of perfect lyrics or even of invariably successful statements. Here, as elsewhere in this final phase, many individual poems suffer from the aim or thesis of the whole. Lyrical quality and even formal design are often sacrificed to the obtrusive urgency with which ideas or doctrines are expounded. Hence a certain solidity of matter, a heaviness of gait and a tendency to repeat themes and phrases ineffectually. And yet what signs of energy, of wide curiosity, of courage, sympathy and faith! The subjects, when not personal, are universal in scope: the history of art, the evolution of love, the phases of power, the development of women, the forces of industry, the progress of science with, as counterparts, a criticism of revealed religion and a vision of the social ideal. Such topics are handled in the free odal form, sometimes with almost epic power and breadth. The lyrical balance is maintained by the passionate 'Cris de ma vie'. And the main purpose of the series is to assert through a study of human development–for the tumultuous forces are pride, will, joy, effort, love, justice–the potential omnipotence of man and the high destiny of the race. The most extensive of Verhaeren's major collections is dedicated to Rodin. But it is significant that while Verhaeren can suggest attitudes of energy and heroism that remind us of some of Rodin's figures, he shows us nothing comparable to the Burghers of Calais.

Following the author of *La Légende des siècles*, he makes a symbolical selection among the operative forces in history. It is hardly a valid criticism to say that his choice is no more representative than Hugo's, since his canvas is so much less extensive. But his effort to fill historical gaps with pieces of rhymed chronology is as laborious as Hugo's example seems to us now. The Flemish poet recovers intensity and interest when he touches the instinctive core of life. Among the longer poems the lament for the passing of Venus ('L'Amour') and the first of the trilogy on women (L'Eternelle')—a remarkable piece of instinctive psychology—are the most attractive. The rest of the volume I would exchange for the penultimate piece called 'Un Soir', one of the most distinctive of Verhaeren's later poems often referred to under the title of its first line:

Celui qui me lira dans les siècles, un soir . . .

The phase of enthusiasm is reflected most fully in *La Multiple Splendeur*. Here, we might say, the power of admiration becomes aware of its ethical potential. Having come to regard admiration as the religious faculty in man, Verhaeren was conscious that, in the life around him, it was this faculty which, more than any other, lacked cultivation and expression. The positive value of contemporary life was for him diminished and its effectiveness impaired by the fanatical cult of the critical spirit which emphasized distinctions and bred hostilities. To react against the disintegrating tendencies of the age by proclaiming an ethical doctrine of fervour now seemed his task as a poet:

Il faut admirer tout pour s'exalter soi-même.

The new series which presents and illustrates the creed was to have born for title the injunction: 'Admirez-vous les uns, les autres'. Its formulation in a number of earnest and ingratiating appeals imposes a crowning unity on the speculative diversity of this final phase.

It was when writing up his impressions of the Paris Exhibition of 1900 that Verhaeren had asked himself whether enthusiasm for the greatness of man as revealed in his struggles and achievements could not be made the basis for a new social ethic. 'The idea comes to us naturally', he wrote in the *Mercure de France*, 'at the sight of this huge concourse of efforts, achievements and victories that constitute a universal exhibition'. He applied it first to nations and recommended mutual admiration as a solvent for international misunderstandings and strife. Turning to individuals he said: 'The respect for life with all its consequences will proceed from the admiration of life. Every man is a masterpiece, even the most ungainly . . . Beauty clothes the whole of life, whether of animals, plants or trees, so effectively that the universal bonds which proceed from her envelop the entire earth. Admiration is the leverage of universal consciousness'.

A faith of this kind expands in *La Multiple Splendeur* into a Magnificat of the whole of creation. The words admire! exalt! ring out in a strain of praise which alternates with the call for a life of sympathy and tolerance, charity and appreciation. This appeal supplies a new standpoint from which the poet can restate his favourite themes: the marvels of industry, the victories of science, the achievements of western civilization. The series ends with a triumphal ode to manual labour which reveals a robust, spontaneous sympathy for all types and grades of humble workers as well as a sense of the dynamic beauty of muscular energy ('L'Effort').

Some of these poems also record the last step in the worship of nature. In *Les Visages de la vie* the physical universe had been, for the most part, a source of sensation and experience. It has now become, as well, an object of love and meditation. The poet exults in its strength and beauty, proclaims its splendours, calls men to admire what he adores, to experience what he has felt. Some of the titles are significant–'A la gloire des cieux', 'A la gloire des vents', 'La Louange du corps humain'–three hymns of praise, of which the first and third are superb examples of the poet's inspired materialism, spiritualized through his perception of beauty.

The sense of personal identification with the universe, which was one of Verhaeren's supreme experiences, is rendered objectively in the noble poem, 'La Louange du corps humain'. Something deeper than philosophic materialism appears in the lines that describe the women whose bodies gleam through the foliage as 'des fragments magnifiques du monde'. This was Verhaeren's serious faith. When he called his own limbs branches, and his fingers leaves, he was not merely indulging in metaphor; he was expressing what was for him a universal truth: we are all parts of nature, even the soul:

> L'âme de flamme et d'or qui brûle en vos cerveaux
> N'est qu'un aspect complexe et fin de la nature.

But the soul, thus defined, is still superior to nature. The poet's religion converges finally upon the worship of the mind as the highest thing we can positively say we know, the sole particle of the material world that has risen to the dignity of self-consciousness and self-direction:

> Cerveau, tu règne seul sur nos actes lucides.

But to exchange our commentary for the poet's résumé, let us turn to the succinct application of his philosophy to poetry which he made in an interview. 'Poetry', he said, 'seems to me bound to end before long in a lucid pantheism. More and more minds that are sane and honest admit the unity of the world. The old divisions between the soul and the body, between God and the Universe are being effaced. Man is a fragment of the world's architecture. He is the consciousness and the intelligence of the whole of which he is a part . . . He is becoming in a sense, by dint of prodigies, the personal God in whom his ancestors believed'.

From the elevated standpoint of the ethic of admiration Verhaeren made a final survey of human endeavour. In 1910 appeared *Les Rythmes souverains*. It would be very inadequate to characterize this volume which contains some of his finest poems as the last restatement of his philosophy. The superior, objective style and more careful form of most of these poems are their distinctive merits. But let us glance first at the moral aspect of the series and the completion it brings to its predecessors.

Verhaeren described the purpose of this series (in a conversation with the present writer in 1914) as an attempt to look through legend and history and select from the most characteristic myths and events those which he could use to illustrate and aggrandize individual effort or collective achievement –those significant gestures which justify the sentiment of admiration and inspire a sense of the greatness and beauty of human effort. To revert to the primitive meaning of the word, the series recounts the *gesta* of humanity in the course of its long ascent and aims at being a kind of *chanson de geste* with mankind as hero and the universe as background. The resemblance to Hugo's intention in writing *La Légende des siècles* is obvious and yet not obtrusive. In scope and variety Verhaeren's final collections cannot be compared with Hugo's vast series, and they reveal a different symbolic emphasis. It was bold of Hugo's *fils sauvage* to emulate his predecessor's adaptation of the legend of Eden in 'Le Sacre de la femme'. But I think comparison would show that in 'Le Paradis' Verhaeren created a myth which has its own strength of meaning and grandeur of form. Hugo's theme is the intimation of Eve's motherhood; Verhaeren's the exclusion from Paradise of the parents of Freedom. Hugo's poem is the more purely lyrical, Verhaeren's the more thoughtful.

Even more recurrent than the word 'geste' in these poems is the word 'rythme' and this implies a differentiation. Life

47

and the universe are perceived no longer in terms of force but of movement. Each subject or episode is treated as the expression of an essential rhythm and is realized in an independent form of beauty, no longer as part of an ideological argument. Some of the best pieces are symbolic narratives adapted from Greek mythology, the resources of which Verhaeren uses for the first time. They show with an accession of strength a new restraint in tone, a firmer relief of outline and a surer feeling for plastic form, even when the vehicle is the *vers libre* as in the magnificent poem, 'Hercule'. Above all these pieces are free from the more aggressive mannerisms of the earlier phases. And although some of the more personal features are lacking–especially the torrential vehemence–they acquire something of the perfection, serenity and harmony of the classical ideal, to whose models and standards many of the verslibrists of the beginning of this century tended to revert. It is significant too that here the twelve-syllable line predominates, as it does in the poet's last play, *Hélène de Sparte*, to a greater degree than in any but the earliest of his productions. The last of the great series prompts the question whether Verhaeren had not come to feel that the sovereign rhythms were, after all, those tested and consecrated by long and noble usage from Ronsard to Corneille, and from Racine to Victor Hugo and Leconte de Lisle.

EPILOGUE

In one of the last poems which he may have read in proof but could not have seen collected, Verhaeren wrote:

Vous m'êtes tous tributaires devant le temps.

The reference is modest, to the manual workers whose efforts he was fond of extolling. But it might legitimately be transferred to many of the poets who succeeded him. Reading his work through again, one can see his debts accumulate to Baudelaire, Rimbaud, Verlaine and Laforgue, to say nothing of Hugo whom he cultivated increasingly. But one also perceives how much in subsequent poetry is latent in the long and varied sequence of his experiments. Here I shall be concerned not to demonstrate influences but simply to indicate a few of the premonitions and prototypes of recent trends discernible in the work of a poet who had impressed critics before 1914 as an audacious innovator.

To begin with his first distinctive phase, Verhaeren's success in making poetry 'out of the complaining voices of the nerves', as Symons put it; his effort to match with imagery and rhythm those 'abysms of melancholy' from which, in Valéry's opinion, he must have suffered acutely, predate an unprecedented invasion of literature and the arts by irrational and neurotic types of fantasy, some of which may strike us as brilliant and revealing, while others leave us indifferent to their trivial and humourless extravagances. Cultivated most feverishly in France, such preoccupations have turned many writers and artists of talent from the time-honoured task of creating beauty to the intuitive analysis, through their special media, of ever more extreme forms of mental and moral aberration.

And here we should remind ourselves that in the middle years of his productivity Verhaeren, still prone to sombre hallucinations, practised what I have ventured to call the modern macabre style—that morbid blend of the grotesque and the corrupt which he took over, with elaborations of his own, from Baudelaire and Huysmans, combining with it elements derived from eccentric artists in the pictorial traditions with which he remained in creative contact. The originality of this composite style lies in the manner of its adaptation to actual situations, and at that Verhaeren could be strangely successful. His numerous experiments in the macabre may be found to have supplied important links between the distortions of late mediaeval and baroque art and the curiosities of contemporary fantasy.

At this point a distinction must be made to avoid misrepresentation. Although his work abounds in material for the psychologist, Verhaeren does not appear to have been touched by Freudian theories. For this reason and also because he was at all times consciously an artist, producing work which, despite the *sauvagerie* of his temperament and the 'paroxysms' of his manner, never ceased to be effectively composed and 'controlled', he cannot be classed as a forerunner of those enemies of logic and artifice, the Surrealists, nor would it be wise to suggest that they felt any curiosity for his work.

Yet, with no desire to force a comparison, one cannot help detecting the recurrence of a certain tone in Verhaeren's phase of distress which becomes resonant in theirs, a distraught note, alien to harmony, balance or repose, which suggests that he too had moments of ominous perception into the confusions of his time, such as the Surrealists profess to have into the obscure chaos of today.

As for the question of modernity, Verhaeren's position looked secure forty years ago, when it would have seemed rhetorical to ask, was he not the first significant poet of the scientific and industrial era? Today what claims may have been his to originality in this sphere are largely ignored. Yet it was the author of *Les Villes tentaculaires* who, with a skill hitherto without precedent, succeeded in adapting to poetry the real operations of the laboratory, the rebarbative aspects of factory premises and the behaviour of operatives at work, in their relaxations and in revolt. He ruminated over the purposes of such activities and strove to appreciate their significance. Since his time the attitude of poets and artists has changed from one of confidence to one of distrust and foreboding. 'When I am in the company of scientists', wrote W. H. Auden recently, 'I feel like a curate who has strayed into a drawing-room full of dukes. If the attitude of poets towards our civilization is merely negative, this is mainly because they know that poets can do nothing to solve the problem of a machine culture and the people who might be able to do so seem hardly aware that these problems exist'. That looks like a failure of nerve. Actually, however, many poets and artists, including Auden, are anxiously concerned with our machine age, its conditions and its culture; and if their approach seems more cautious than Verhaeren's it is because they have reason to be more suspicious. Yet none appear to have advanced beyond him in the attempt to solve the technical problem involved in making lyrical reference to the implements and products of an aggressive materialism, which has revolutionized our social life and opened before it simultaneous prospects of power and disaster. It may be that contemporary poets are more indebted to his example than they are aware of being. I have disclaimed any intention of 'proving' influences. But anyone who has studied the way a literary influence works knows that it can affect subsequent writers without deliberate effort on their part and often despite a healthy disregard for precedents. I see little in contemporary poetry of a similar inspiration that surpasses Verhaeren's in ingenuity. Yet how often the relationship of science to poetry is discussed without mention being made of the name of a poet in whose work the long line of what in France has been called *la poésie scientifique* had reached a resounding ascendency before the end of last century. What Verhaeren achieved was not merely the appropriation of the nomenclature of apparatus and experiment and its adaptation in neat catalogues of rhymed description; much of that kind had been done before him. He abandoned the age-long practice of personifying natural forces and dramatizing their interactions. Instead, he adopted the terms by which science identifies forces and substances in the laboratory and in the lecture-room. Marinetti is said to have claimed Verhaeren as the 'spiritual father' of the school he founded. But it is hardly a compliment to his experimental mannerisms to say that they served as models for the imitative frivolities of Futurism. A real fervour inspires the best of his modernist verse. Arbitrary details and operations become poetical through the feeling he has for them, and description is caught up and galvanized in the energy of his rhythms and images.

An anecdote may illustrate his attitude. During the first world war Verhaeren made a tour of the Welsh colleges, where he spoke on behalf of his country. It was my luck to accompany him. As we set out I intimated that there might be something down the line to interest the author of *Les Villes tentaculaires*. But I was hardly prepared for the poet's reaction as the descent towards Landore expanded into one of the most spectacular industrial landscapes he had ever beheld.

Today Landore is losing its picturesqueness; recent processes of readaptation have tempered the infernal character of its surroundings and have removed much of the débris left from savage exploitation. But on that afternoon in November 1914 foundries and furnaces were in full blast, surcharging with smoke and flame an atmosphere of copper-bound fog. Obscurely lit by the strangled glow of a sun setting far across the bay, the prospect was, in the grandest modern manner, apocalyptic. And the poet whose speciality it had been to match such effects with words responded without restraint to the spectacle. From window to window he rushed, his arms held up in amazement, as if he were possessed by a kind of sacred terror, transforming the scene with his vision and reiterating an irrepressible phrase –unpardonable perversity or significant paradox?–*Que c'est beau! Que c'est beau!*

In one of the most significant short poems of his later period –'Le Navire' (*Les Rythmes souverains*)–humanity is symbolized as a ship being steered by its captain over the troubled seas of time into the serenity of the future:

> Il tanguait sur l'effroi, la mort et les abîmes,
> D'accord avec chaque astre et chaque volonté,
> Et, maîtrisant ainsi les forces unanimes,
> Semblait dompter et s'asservir l'éternité.

Here in the recognition of the unanimity of natural operations, the gradual advance in man's perception of their laws and his progressive adaptation of life to their sanctions, we recognize the basic principles and inspiration of the movement called Unanimism. From the tentative experiments of 1906 made by the group of L'Abbaye, and soon to be followed by the theories and applications of M. Jules Romains, poetry, drama and the novel in France have been periodically refreshed by a type of initiative which owes part of its impulse to the original examples of Whitman and Verhaeren.

The war of 1914 was an acid solvent for much in the genial faith in comradeship propagated by the Unanimists. When peace at last succeeded four years of automatic slaughter, two new phenomena began to exert diverse attractions of great potency, the psychological revelation of Freud and the poetical revelation of Mr Eliot.

The term 'modern', so much abused in Verhaeren's connection, is but a relative qualification. For most of us today, the epoch of modern poetry dates from the appearance in 1922 of *The Waste Land*, or perhaps one should say, from the gradual realization in the ensuing decade of the significance of this difficult poem. What Verhaeren had in common with the Unanimists, namely collective vision and humanitarian sympathies, separated him from Eliot, whose deeper analysis–psychological in character and metaphysical in judgment–proved to be more satisfying to the intelligentsia of a world recovering from the unprecedented wastage of the biggest war in history. Strong new movements in literature and the arts can effect such diversions and achieve such injustices. Yet it is not improbable that the fuliginous tableaux of *Les Villes tentaculaires* had impressed thoughtful readers at the turn of the century with as deep a sense of cleavage in the modern soul as that which Eliot's poem exposed through a different approach and technique.

Valéry, in his admirable discourse, makes a vital distinction which should be noticed here. 'Until Verhaeren', he says, 'poetry had done nothing but skim all subjects which the life of our time, mechanized and brutal, powerful yet enslaved, proposes to the wonder, horror, anger and aspiration of men. Modern man has put his greatness outside himself. On the world which contains him and of which he is an infinitesimal part and an ephemeral production, he had for a century been carrying on an immense task of artificial transformation, the limits and consequences of which he cannot foresee.

'Yet through his memories and his instincts and by all that is most tender and intimate in him, this same man still belongs to the world of nature, to a world once virgin and which formerly contained nothing but spontaneous phenomena. Man is thus divided against himself; he finds himself powerful yet wretched, unequal to his triumphs, and, as it were, a stranger in this new situation, this order which he nevertheless has made with his own hands and which is the result of his researches, his calculations, his inflexible will to knowledge and to power.

'We are living through a great drama,' Valéry continues, 'a drama that has found its poet. The motifs of this life divided between what has been and what is becoming, the spectacle of this disturbance of nature and of the insensate activity of men have found in Verhaeren a master capable of presenting them and their unique singer. Through him our material civilization has received the eminent dignity of lyrical expression.'

The memory of the great Belgian poet whose bust in the place St. Séverin at Paris was unveiled on the occasion when these words were spoken has received no finer tribute. It brings

53

us to our last question. How is our subject related to the dominant philosophical mood of today?

Verhaeren was no metaphysical; yet like some of our prominent metaphysicians he could not have placed essence before existence. If to be an existentialist meant to believe in life and to enjoy it, then he would be the greatest existential poet. But he is merely a great singer of existence, and so for the moment his message is effaced by a type of philosophy which recommends life with a grimace of courage, as if it were largely repulsive. His insistence on *orgueil* (self-reliance) and freedom has all the force which the Existentialists attach to these words —without the desperation. His recommendation of existence is a benediction:

> Et que la vie avec ses ouragans déments
> Vous reste chère immensément,
> Ainsi qu'une admirable et tragique conquête.

The resemblance to Nietzsche's 'religious affirmations of life, of the whole of life, not of denied or partial life', will occur to the reader; although Verhaeren (in a conversation with the present writer) rejected the implication that he had been influenced by the idea of the Superman. Like Nietzsche, however, he had a strong sense of the tragic heroism involved in the acceptance of necessity. The supreme courage of the exceptional being who pits all the strength of his physical, mental and moral faculties against the overwhelming powers of circumstance stirred the poet to his depths, especially at the moment of paroxysm, when nerves and sinews are strained to the utmost and the magnificent rage of humain despair closes in conflict with the obscure violence of human destiny:

> La force la plus belle est la force qui pleure.

But what of the tragedies involved in the common human lot of our time? The author of *Les Villes tentaculaires* sees soundness of life frustrated, beauty desecrated and innocence befouled in conditions where

> Un nouvel être naît: homme, enfant, vieillard, femme,
> Tordus en total noir, en somme infâme . . .

But as with many benevolent observers in the days of pre-war prosperity, his sense of menace tends to evaporate in the assumption that all things work together for good in accordance with 'l'instinct mieux défini de l'être humain', which laws are gradually being disclosed by science. Complacency is the last failing of which a mind and heart as sensitive and noble as Verhaeren's could be accused. It is none the less disturbing to find how completely the denunciations of *Les Villes tentaculaires* fade into the acclamations of the later volumes–save for the references to war which, like a thunderbolt falling from skies that seemed blue, shook the refugee profoundly but could hardly be said to have renewed the poet's inspiration.

More seriously still, like many another pantheist, Verhaeren shows no sense of the tragic mystery of evil, that inveterate perversity which Baudelaire perceived and denounced in himself and in other men. The later poet's genuine naïveté is here at a discount; he does not seem to have realized either the unaccountable malignancy of wickedness or its tenacious subtlety and resource. It stands, no doubt, to the honour of his fundamental sanity and reverence that Verhaeren betrays no prescience of the horrors of forced labour, organized torture and mass murder on the scale of unprecedented magnitude which many of his younger contemporaries lived to suffer or to witness within a few decades of his death. And it may go far to explain the relative neglect of his work to admit that while we may have no more conviction than he had of a personal deity we have none of his confidence in the divinization of man through science:

> Celui qui prouve et sait vaincra celui qui croit . . .
> Et le monde roulé dans les métamorphoses,
> Après avoir eu foi en Dieu, croira en soi.

Still less may we be able to believe in the solution of the mystery of God, which he outlined in these words: 'Although sceptical and very hesitant in matters of belief, I never doubt one thing, that the *savants* will succeed–though I don't know when–in unveiling the real significance of life, in giving us the true understanding of the universe, the veritable knowledge of God. I am entirely, absolutely convinced of that'.

Adapting a phrase of Peter Quennell's, T. S. Eliot differentiated the kind of poet we need when he said of Baudelaire that he had the 'sense of the age'. How does Verhaeren meet this criterion? 'Our entire epoch is reflected in his work', said Stefan

Zweig. But had Verhaeren the critical attitude which Eliot found in Baudelaire, and which we find in Eliot and in the later poems of Yeats? Verhaeren saw with incomparable breadth what Zweig again called 'all manifestations of the modernity of his day'. But did he see *through* them? Let us recall Baudelaire's famous theory of civilization: 'It is not in gas or in steam or in turning tables. It is in the diminution of the traces of original sin'. We must not of course expect theological discriminations from Verhaeren. But has he any criticism of comparable depth to offer? Such questions are unavoidable. They suggest that a large part of his report, for all its vivid realism, is not profoundly penetrating. No poetry is more vitalistic than his, but no vitalistic poetry was ever less complete as a criticism of life. Its moral stimulation is real, but it is an encouragement rather than a cure. To say this is not to suggest that it has no lasting virtues. Verhaeren knew where the permanence of his poetry lay. And this brings us back to the best of his poems, to one like 'Un Soir' (already referred to), a poem true to the aspirations of his time and to whose exultant sympathy and assurance the future can scarcely be unresponsive—if it resembles the beauty of his hope:

Celui qui me lira dans les siècles, un soir,
Troublant mes vers, sous leur sommeil ou sous leur cendre,
Et ranimant leur sens lointain pour mieux comprendre
Comment ceux d'aujourd'hui s'étaient armés d'espoir,

Qu'il sache, avec quel violent élan, ma joie
S'est, à travers les cris, les révoltes, les pleurs,
Ruée au combat fier et mâle des douleurs,
Pour en tirer l'amour, comme on conquiert sa proie . . .

Une tendresse énorme emplit l'âpre savoir,
Il exalte la force et la beauté des mondes,
Il devine les liens et les causes profondes;
O vous qui me lirez, dans les siècles, un soir,

Comprenez-vous pourquoi mon vers vous interpelle?
C'est qu'en vos temps quelqu'un d'ardent aura tiré
Du cœur de la nécessité même, le vrai,
Bloc clair, pour y dresser l'entente universelle.

APPENDIX

Translations of passages quoted in the text

p. 7. Future, you exalt me as God did formerly.

p. 11. On the horizon, where the long roads lose themselves in the direction of dawn, there float by the light of the stubble and to the sough of the wind, phantom forms which skim the turf with their hovering feet.

For it's the hour when, far off, the Angels, in garlands, come down to gather, in melancholy wise, along the plains of the mute air, the sleeping lily, the supernatural lily, that blooms in legend.

p. 13. Who could have predicted, O God! that one day sad dawn would find echoless that sonorous lyre whose sweet songs soothed our century at its birth? Who would have said that my heart in its impotent flight would, like the dove sent to the deluge, seek in vain through the world for a green branch, and come for shelter to the sad refuge of the Muses' temple, open to all the winds?

p. 14. So also in my heart where the terror of doubt . . .

p. 16. 'the wenches'.
Craesbeke, Brakenburgh, Teniers, Dusart, Brauwer
With Steen, the fattest, the most drunken, in the centre.

p. 17. ... the terrible drama of the black, godless century does not damage their faith.

p. 20. Ah, how dolorous was that opaque evening when my soul, undermined by infinite doubt, collapsed entire, splitting my will with a dark crevice.

p. 22. By exacerbating the heart's ills one commands them.

Nothing, neither heroes nor new saviours, and we remain wallowing in native reason.

I will stride towards madness and its suns, its white moon-suns at midday, bizarre.

Hallucinate me with thy absurdity; and crown me thy king, suffering and ridiculous.

p. 23. The winter night lifts to heaven its pure chalice.
And I too lift my heart, my nocturnal heart, O Lord! my heart, my heart, to Thy void infinite. And yet I know that all is taciturn and that what my heart dies athirst of does not exist. And I know Thee a lie; yet my lips pray and my knees. I know Thy great hands shut, Thy great eyes closed to those who cry in despair, and that it is I who alone dream myself into things. Have pity, Lord, on my entire distress. Needs must I offer my affliction with tears to Thy silence.
The winter night lifts to heaven its pure chalice.

Quays and barracks; endless quays and their lanterns spinning, immobile and slow, the dark golds of their lights; dreary (processions) of stones, houses of brick, towers of darkness, whose panes open like grim eyelids in the evening fog; vast docks of maddening toil, full of dismantled ships, their yards quartered against a sky of crucifixion.

In its robe of dead jewels, solemnized by the hour of the purple horizon, the corpse of my reason trails down the Thames.

p. 25. Say, towards what wild unknown, and towards what somnambulent awakenings, and towards what beyonds and towards what convulsionary suns, wherever they may be?

Skull, rich skull, do you hear Folly hovering?

p. 26. Cool place of sojourn where the tempest of my reason, gliding away with the flow of my blood, came to rest.

p. 28. Terrifying, affrighted. He sought the road that leads to another existence bursting into miracles in a desert of rocks illuminated with oracles, where the oak would live, where bronze would speak.

Sing all my voices of hope! Sing within me; sing under the boughs along paths full of sunlight! Micas of silver, stand for joy among the stones; and you, white pebbles of the waters, open your eyes in the brooks through the water of your eyelids; landscape, with thy vermeil lakes, be the mirror of the flaming flight of St. George towards my soul!

p. 30. The windows and the dials with their large gaping eyes witnessed the ruin of his ardour; but the tenacious old ferryman kept, all the same, till God knows when, the green reed between his teeth.

p. 32. With their cat, with their dog, with their bird in a cage, with one means only of keeping alive: drink one's bane, check one's rage; footsore and mouldy at heart, the folk hereabouts, leaving their haunts and countrysides, set off tonight along the roads to the infinite.

p. 33. Formidable and criminal, the arms of hyperbolical machines, mowing down the evangelical corn, have frightened off the old melancholy sower whose gestures seemed in accord with heaven.

p. 34. O the centuries and centuries on this town! Great in its past, ceaselessly ardent–and traversed as now by phantoms!

Teeming city, city full of dreams, where the spectre in full daylight clutches the passer-by!

Towards one knows not what disquieting goals?

p. 35. Tragic, black and legendary, with gluey feet and wild gestures, Death sweeps the whole town into a great hole in the cemetery.

With eyes meticulous or monstrous, one detects increases and disasters mounting from atoms up to stars. Life, immense and solidary, is there examined in its surface or in its miraculous folds, as the sea and its surging gulfs are probed by the myriad golden hands of the sun.

Each one toils with avidity, methodically slow, in a combined effort; each one unties a knot in the complexity of the problems that are assembled there; and all examine, watch and prove, all are right—but only one finds!

p. 36. . . . . the synthesis of the worlds!

It's the house of science darting towards the unity of all ideas.

O human race linked to the stars of gold, hast thou felt with what formidable, battering toil, suddenly in a century thy immense strength is shaken? . . . The spirit of the country was the spirit of God; it feared research and revolt, it fell; and now it dies under the axles and fiery wains of new harvests.

p. 37 My heart, a burning bush, has set my lips on fire.

The desperate effort to weigh all, to know all, probes the dense, moving forest of living things. And despite the brushwood in which some steps become ensnared, man conquers his law of rights and duties.

p. 38. If suddenly my adventurous soul leaps towards the future, at once I feel again, as I did in my childhood, the sleeping wing of former prayers quiver in the depth of me . . .
O ancient hearth whose spark survives! O upright prayer! O new prayer! Future, you exalt me as formerly God did; you also dominate the hour and age we live in; but you, at least, one day you'll become men and be their minds, their brows, their arms, their eyes.
Were you to be less than my dream desires, what matters it if each time my ardour catches sight of you it kindles and revives . . .

p. 40. The fair garden, flowered with flames, which seemed to us the double or the mirror of the bright garden we carry in our souls.

p. 41. Multiply and surrender yourself, dispense your being in a million beings; and feel immensity with its calm or its terror filter and merge so powerfully and deeply into you that the winds and storms absorb you . . .

p. 42. Fusion was born through a love of things so simple and violent that I no longer felt my heart beat save to the flow and ebb of deep metamorphoses: I found my hands and arms again in the branches and tendrils of the ripe vines; the hill itself was sculptured in the bloc of my will: I became intoxicated with their ample, mutual life, and my five senses prolonged themselves so far and so deep in it that it seemed to burn and ferment with all my blood.

p. 45. He who reads me one evening in centuries to come . . .

One must admire all to become exalted oneself.

p. 46. The soul of flame and gold that burns in your brains is but a complex and refined aspect of nature.

Brain, you alone rule our lucid acts.

p. 49 You are all my tributaries before (the bar of) time.

p. 52. It tossed over terrors, death and abysses, in accord with every star and every will, and mastering thus the unanimous forces, seemed to subdue eternity and make it serve itself.

p. 54. And may life with its demented hurricanes remain immensely dear to you as an admirable and tragic conquest.

The finest strength is the strength that weeps.

A new being is born: man, child, old man, woman, wrung out of total blackness, in a word, vile . . .

p. 55. He who proves and knows will conquer him who believes . . . and the world rolling through its metamorphoses, after having had faith in God, will believe in itself.

p. 56. He who reads me one evening in centuries to come, disturbing my verses under their sleep or their dust and reviving their far-off meaning the better to understand how men of today had armed themselves with hope, let him know with what violent impulse my joy has rushed, through cries, revolts and tears, into the proud, virile combat with suffering, so as to draw therefrom love, as one conquers one's prey . . . An enormous tenderness floods the harshness of science. It exalts the strength and beauty of the worlds; it discerns the bonds and deep causes (of things); O you who will read me one evening in centuries to come, do you grasp why my verses call out to you? It is because in your time some ardent spirit will have drawn from the heart of necessity itself the truth, a clear block on which to build universal understanding.

BIOGRAPHICAL NOTES

1855, 21 May:	Birth at Saint-Amand near Antwerp.
1866:	First Communion (18 March). Sent as boarder to Institute of Saint Louis at Brussels.
1868, Sept.:	Transferred to Jesuit College of Sainte-Barbe at Gand.
1874, Oct.:	Becomes law-student at University of Louvain.
1874:	First piece of writing, 'Plus de Poètes', published in *Revue générale* (Brussels).
1881:	Obtains degree of Doctor of Laws (Louvain) and is articled to the barrister, Edmond Picard of Brussels.
1883, 1 Feb.:	Publication of first volume of poems, *Les Flamandes*.
1887:	Publication of *Les Soirs*, inspired by a nervous breakdown.
1891, 24 Aug.:	Marriage to Marthe Massin.
1896, 24 Feb.:	Banquet at Hôtel Métropole, Brussels.
1899:	The poet and his wife go to reside at Saint-Cloud. They also acquire a small house at Caillou-qui-bique, in Hainaut.
1900, 29 Feb.:	First presentation of *Le Cloître* at the Théâtre du Parc, Brussels, and at the Théâtre de l'Œuvre, Paris.
1901, 31 May:	*Les Aubes* played at Section de l'Art of the Maison du Peuple, Brussels.
1912, 4 May:	First presentation of *Hélène de Sparte* at Théâtre du Châtelet, Paris. Lecture tour in Switzerland.
1913, Dec.:	Lecture tour in Russia: Saint Petersburg and Moscow.
1914, Oct.:	The poet and his wife received as refugees in England and Wales.
1916, 27 Nov.:	Fatal accident in Rouen station. The poet's last words: 'Ma femme, ma patrie'.
1917:	Royal Society of Literature: Verhaeren Commemoration, addresses by E. Gosse, Delchevalerie, Hymans and Robert Bridges.
1927:	Ceremony of inauguration of the tomb at Saint-Amand.
1927, 10 Nov.:	Unveiling of bust in the Place Saint-Séverin, Paris. Oration by Paul Valéry.

LIST OF PUBLISHED WORKS

1883:   *Les Flamandes*, poems. Brussels, L. Hochsteyn.
1885:   *Les Contes de minuit*, prose. Brussels, J. Franck.
1885:   *Joseph Heymans*, criticism. Brussels, F. Larcier.
*1886:   *Les Moines*, poems. Paris, Alphonse Lemerre.
1887:   *Les Soirs*, poems. Brussels, E. Deman.
1888:   *Les Débâcles*, poems. Brussels, E. Deman.
1890:   *Les Flambeaux noirs*, poems. Brussels, E. Deman.
1891:   *Au Bord de la route*, poems. Liége, Vaillant-Carmaune.
1891:   *Les Apparus dans mes chemins*, poems. Brussels, Lacomblez.
1893:   *Les Campagnes hallucinées*, poems. Brussels, E. Deman.
*1895:   *Les Villages illusoires*, poems. Brussels, E. Deman.
1895:   *Les Villes tentaculaires*, poems. Brussels, E. Deman.
1896:   *Les Heures claires*, poems. Brussels, E. Deman.
1898:   *Les Aubes*, drama in verse and prose. Brussels, E. Deman.
1899:   *Les Visages de la vie*, poems. Brussels, E. Deman.
1899:   *España Negra*, prose, trans. by Dario de Regoyos. Barcelona, Pedro Ortega.
1899:   *Les Vignes de ma muraille*, included in *Poèmes IIIᵉ série*. Paris, Mercure de France.
1900:   *Le Cloître*, drama in verse and prose. Brussels, E. Deman.
1900:   *Petites Légendes*, poems. Brussels, E. Deman.
1901:   *Philippe Deux*, *épisode dramatique* in verse and prose. Paris, Mercure de France.
1901:   *Les Petits Vieux*, poem. London, Hacon and Ricketts.
1902:   *Les Forces tumultueuses*, poems. Paris, Mercure de France.
1904:   *Toute la Flandre, Les Tendresses premières*, poems. Brussels, E. Deman.
1905:   *Les Heures d'après-midi*, poems. Brussels, E. Deman.
1905:   *Rembrandt, biographie critique*. Paris, Henri Laurens.
1906:   *La Mutiple Splendeur*, poems. Paris, Mercure de France.
1906:   *Images japonaises*, verses with illustrations by Kwassou. Tokio, T. Haségawa.
1907:   *Toute la Flandre, La Guirlande des dunes*, poems. Brussels, E. Deman.
1907:   *Les Lettres françaises en Belgique*, prose. Brussels, Lamertin.
1908:   *Toute la Flandre, Les Héros*, poems. Brussels, E. Deman.
1908:   *James Ensor*, criticism. Brussels, Van Oest.
1908:   *Les Visages de la vie, Les Douze Mois*, poems. Paris, Mercure de France.
1909:   *Toute la Flandre, Les Villes à pignons*, poems. Brussels, E. Deman.
1909:   *Helenas Heimkehr*, trans. by Stefan Zweig of *Hélène de Sparte*. Leipzig, Insel-Verlag.
1910:   *Les Rythmes souverains*, poems. Paris, Mercure de France.
1910:   *Pierre-Paul Rubens*, study. Brussels, Van Oest.
1911:   *Les Heures du soir*, poems. Leipzig, Insel-Verlag.
1911:   *Toute la Flandre, Les Plaines*, poems. Brussels, E. Deman.
1912:   *Hélène de Sparte*, tragedy in verse. Paris, Nouvelle Revue française.
1912:   *Les Blés mouvants*, poems. Paris, Crès.
1915:   *La Belgique sanglante*, prose. Paris, Mercure de France.
1916:   *Les Ailes rouges de la guerre*, poems. Paris, Mercure de France.
1916:   *Parmi les cendres*, prose. Paris, Crès.
1916:   *Villes meurtries de Belgique*, prose. Brussels and Paris, Van Oest.
1916:   *Poèmes légendaires de Flandre et de Brabant*. Paris, Société littéraire de France.
1917:   *Les Flammes hautes*, poems. Paris, Mercure de France.
1920:   *Cinq récits*, gravés par Frans Masereel. Geneva, Le Sablier.
1923:   *A la vie qui s'éloigne*, poems. Paris, Mercure de France.

1926: *Impressions*, 1re série. Paris, Mercure de France. (Second and third series, 1927 and '28.)

1937: *A Marthe Verhaeren*, 219 letters edited by R. Vandevoir. Paris, Mercure de France.

The Mercure de France has published a complete edition of the *Œuvres* in nine volumes.

* In later editions of these volumes, the date of the year previous to that of publication is prefixed to the poems.

SELECT BIBLIOGRAPHY

Baudouin, L. C.: *Le Symbole chez E. V. Essai de psychanalyse de l'art*, 1925.

Estève, E.: *Un grand poète de la vie moderne*, 1929.

Hellens, F.: *Emile Verhaeren*, 1952. (Recommended.)

Jones, P. M.: *E.V. A Study in the Development of his Art and Ideas*, 1926. (Parts of the first chapter and much of the sixth in the present essay are adapted from this work.)

Mockel, A.: *E. V., poète de l'énergie*, 1910.

Morier, H.: *Le Rythme du vers libre symboliste*. I. Verhaeren, 1943.

Poncheville, A. M. de: *Vie de Verhaeren*, 1953. (Recommended.)

Sadleir, M.: *Things Past*, 1945. (Contains an attractive impression of the poet at Caillou-qui-bique.)

Saint-Clair, M.: *Il y a quarante ans*, 1936. (Reminiscences of a passionate episode in the poet's life subsequent to his marriage.)

Starkie, E.: *Les Sources du lyrisme dans la poésie d'E. V.*, 1927.

Zweig, S.: *Verhaeren*, English translation by J. Bithell, 1914.